The emerging nonprofit sector
An overview

Nonprofit organizations are playing an increasingly influential role in the economies and societies of countries throughout the world. This book, the product of the most comprehensive international research project on this sector ever undertaken, offers an unparalleled international overview of the scope, structure, financing and role of this emerging nonprofit sector.

The authors provide a comparative analysis of the findings of individual empirical assessments of the scope, structure and financing of the nonprofit sector in twelve countries: the United States, the United Kingdom, France, Germany, Italy, Hungary, Japan, Brazil, Ghana, Egypt, Thailand, and India. They explore the global scale of this sector, its sources of revenue, and differences between the countries analyzed. They evaluate how well-equipped nonprofit organizations are to respond to the shift towards nonprofit action and away from government in many societies, and they identify the key issues such organizations need to address in the future, such as coming to terms with government and improving management.

Lester M. Salamon is Director of the Johns Hopkins Comparative Nonprofit Sector Project, and Professor at The Johns Hopkins University School of Arts and Sciences. Helmut K. Anheier is Associate Director of the Project, a Senior Research Associate of the Institute for Policy Studies, and Associate Professor of Sociology at Rutgers University.

D0043260

Johns Hopkins Nonprofit Sector Series
edited by Lester M. Salamon and Helmut K. Anheier
Institute for Policy Studies, The Johns Hopkins University

Manchester University Press is proud to be publishing this
important new series, the product of the most comprehensive
comparative analysis of the global nonprofit sector ever
undertaken. The growth of the sector between the public and
the private, known variously as the nonprofit, voluntary or
third sector, is one of the most significant contemporary
developments in societies throughout the world. The books in this series
will cover the development and role of this sector in a broad cross-
section of nations, and also provide comparative, cross-
country analyses.

Johns Hopkins Nonprofit Sector Series 1

THE EMERGING NONPROFIT SECTOR

An overview

Lester M. Salamon
and
Helmut K. Anheier

Manchester University Press

Manchester and New York

distributed exclusively in the USA and Canada by St Martin's Press

Copyright © Lester M. Salamon, Johns Hopkins Comparative Nonprofit Sector
Project 1996

Published by Manchester University Press
Oxford Road, Manchester M13 9NR, UK
and Room 400, 175 Fifth Avenue, New York, NY 10010, USA

Distributed exclusively in the USA and Canada
by St Martin's Press, Inc., 175 Fifth Avenue, New York,
NY 10010, USA

British Library Cataloguing-in-Publication Data
A catalogue record for this book is available from the British Library

Library of Congress Cataloging-in-Publication Data
Salamon, Lester M.
    The emerging nonprofit sector : an overview / Lester M. Salamon and
Helmut K. Anheier.
        p.   cm. — (Johns Hopkins nonprofit sector series ; 1)
    Includes bibliographical references.
    ISBN 0–7190–4871–0 (hardback). — ISBN 0–7190–4872–9 (paperback)
    1. Nonprofit organizations.   2. Nongovernmental organizations.
3. Social service.   4. Nonprofit organizations—Employees.   5. Nongovernmental organizations—Employees.   6. Social workers.
7. Volunteers.   I. Anheier, Helmut K., 1954– .   II. Title.
III. Series.
    HD2769. 15.S25   1996
    338.7—dc20   95–21423

ISBN 0 7190 4871 0 *hardback*
     0 7190 4872 9 *paperback*

First published 1994 by Institute for Policy Studies,
The Johns Hopkins University

00 99 98 97 96   10 9 8 7 6 5 4 3 2 1

Printed in Great Britain
by Bell & Bain Ltd, Glasgow

For Dr. Lawrence Atingdui
A dedicated seeker of truth

CONTENTS

vii

Contents

The following signs and conversion rates are used in this book:

billion = thousand million
   · = decimal point
1 ECU = 1.273 U.S.$ (1990)
1 U.S.$ = 0.785 ECU (1990)

LIST OF FIGURES

ix

LIST OF TABLES

SERIES EDITORS' FOREWORD

This book is one in a series of monographs on the voluntary or nonprofit sector throughout the world that have resulted from the *Johns Hopkins Comparative Nonprofit Sector Project*, a major inquiry into the scope, structure, history, legal position, and role of the nonprofit sector in a broad cross-section of nations.

Launched in May 1990, this project has sought to close the glaring gaps in knowledge that have long existed about the thousands of schools, hospitals, clinics, community organizations, advocacy groups, day care centers, relief organizations, nursing homes, homeless shelters, family counseling agencies, environmental groups and others that comprise this important sector. Though known by different names in different places, these organizations are present almost everywhere, albeit to widely differing extents. More than that, there is significant evidence that they are growing considerably in both scope and scale as faith has declined in the capability of government to cope on its own with the interrelated challenges of persistent poverty, environmental degradation, and social change. Indeed, we seem to be in the midst of a global "associational revolution" that is opening new opportunities for organized private action and placing new demands and responsibilities on private not-for-profit groups. As a result, it has becoming increasingly important to understand what the scope and contours of this nonprofit sector really are, and what its potentials are for shouldering the new demands being placed upon it.

The *Johns Hopkins Comparative Nonprofit Sector Project* was conceived as a way to meet this need, to document the scope, structure, revenue base, and background of the nonprofit sector, and

xi

to do so in a way that not only yielded solid and objective information about individual countries, but made it possible to undertake cross-national comparisons in a systematic way. For this purpose, we identified twelve (later thirteen) countries representing different religious and historical traditions, different regions of the world, and different levels of economic development. Included were seven advanced industrial societies (the U.S., U.K., France, Germany, Italy, Sweden, and Japan), five "developing" societies (Brazil, Ghana, Egypt, Thailand, and India), and one former Soviet bloc country (Hungary). In each of these countries we recruited a local associate and undertook a similar set of information-gathering activities guided by a common definition, a common classification scheme, and a common set of data-gathering forms and instructions. The result, we believe, is the first systematic attempt to put the nonprofit sector on the social and economic map of the world in a solid and empirical way.

The present book provides an overview of the major empirical results of this project, primarily for the seven countries in which it was initially possible to gather reliable empirical data (the U.S., the U.K., France, Germany, Italy, Hungary, and Japan). Comparable data were also collected on Sweden, which joined the project a year later than the others, but these data were not available in time for the inclusion in the original edition of this book, which was published by the Johns Hopkins Institute for Policy Studies in 1994.

Among the more salient findings of this project as reported here are these: that the nonprofit sector is a far more significant economic force than has heretofore been acknowledged in countries as diverse as centralized France and Japan and decentralized Germany and the United States; that this sector is highly diverse, with significant involvement in such fields as health, education, arts, and social services, though the exact structure of the sector differs from place to place; and that private giving plays a smaller role, and public sector support and fees a larger role, in the financing of this set of organizations than is widely believed. In the process, the book raises a number of challenges to existing theories about the nonprofit sector and about the evolution of developed and developing societies alike. Against this backdrop, the volume then identifies a number of significant challenges that stand in the way of the further development of this sector at the present time and the implications these have both for nonprofit organizations and the broader societies of which they are a part.

From its outset, the *Johns Hopkins Comparative Nonprofit Sector Project* has been a collaborative effort among an extraordinary group of scholars with support from a wide array of funders and advisors. The team of local associates—Martin Knapp and Jeremy Kendall in the U.K., Edith Archambault in France, Paolo Barbetta and Pippo Ranci in Italy, Helmut Anheier, Eckhard Priller and Wolfgang Seibel in Germany, Éva Kuti in Hungary, Tadashi Yamamoto and Takayoshi Amenomori in Japan, Leilah Landim in Brazil, Lawrence Atingdui and Emmanuel Laryea in Ghana, Amani Kandil in Egypt, Amara Pongsapich in Thailand, Sven-Erik Sjöstrand, Filip Wijkström, and Thomas Lundström in Sweden —has worked together at every stage to perfect the information-gathering forms, develop the basic definitions and classification scheme, and interpret the results. To all of them, we owe a deep debt of gratitude.

Thanks are also due to the numerous individuals who served on the International Advisory Committee to this project, to the members of the national advisory committees we formed to oversee the work, to Richard Purslow of Manchester University Press for the crucial encouragement he has provided in bringing this work to publication, and to the foundations, corporations, and government agencies throughout the world that provided support to make this work possible.

It was more than 150 years ago that the Frenchman Alexis de Toqueville identified the "art of associating together" as the mother of all science. Today we appear to be in the middle of an extraordinary explosion of associational activity as new forms of organized citizen action are taking shape and expanding their role in widely disparate parts of the world. Our hope is that the series of monographs of which this volume is an important part will help make this process of change more visible and more understandable and thereby contribute to its success. We are convinced that important values hinge critically on this result.

L.M.S.
H.K.A.
Baltimore, Maryland
January 1996

PREFACE

Launched in May 1990, the *Johns Hopkins Comparative Nonprofit Sector Project* has engaged the energies of more than 200 people in 13 countries throughout the world, to all of whom I owe a deep debt of gratitude. Prominent among these were a handful of foresighted philanthropic leaders —Sylvie Tsyboula in France; Michael Brophy in the United Kingdom; Akira Iriyama in Japan; Ray Handlan, Benjamin Shute, David Arnold, and Barry Gaberman in the United States; and Horst Niemeyer in Germany— who saw the need for this project early on and who provided critical assistance in generating financial and other support for the endeavor.

In carrying out the project we were aided by an extraordinary network of local associates in the project countries. These individuals, who are listed opposite the title page, worked with us at every stage of the process—to develop our basic definitions and approach, to design the basic information-gathering forms, and ultimately to gather much of the original data reported here. This was a truly cooperative undertaking and the knowledge, insight, hard work, and collaborative spirit that this unusual team of associates brought to the effort, and the additional talents that they in turn mobilized in their respective countries, were crucial to whatever success we have had. Altogether, as reflected in the list opposite the back cover over 50 researchers were actively involved in one aspect or another of this work.

In addition to these direct participants, this project has benefited from the advice and assistance of more than 150 other government and nonprofit leaders around the world who participated on an International Advisory Committee or on separate project advisory committees in the individual countries. The International Advisory Committee, listed opposite the table of contents, assisted in every phase of the effort, from identification of potential sources of support through to designing the dissemination of the results. The country advisory committees provided similar help at the country level, including providing access to national data sources and ensuring sensitivity to national circumstances.

Others who contributed importantly to this project were Marilyn Taylor, who organized a crucial project team meeting in Bristol, England, and helped in many other ways; Russy Sumariwalla, who served on our International Advisory Committee and helped organize a project team meeting in Alexandria, Virginia; Wojciech Sokolowski, Gabriel Rudney, Kusuma Cunningham, Donna Schaub, and Jacquelyn Perry, who provided important research and administrative support for the effort; and John Richardson of the European Foundation Centre, who backed this project from the outset and took on the task of organizing the initial release event.

Finally, this project would not have been possible without the support of numerous organizations listed on the inside of the back cover, which were willing to take a chance on what must have seemed a very speculative undertaking and provided the financial assistance that made this work feasible.

To all of these individuals and organizations, and to our families, who had to put up with the distractions and absences that a project of this scale and complexity inevitably involves, we express our deepest thanks. Responsibility for whatever errors of fact or interpretation remain, however, is ours, and we accept it fully.

This book represents the first in what will be an extended series of publications from this project. A tentative list of titles is included at the end of this report.

This first published product of this project is dedicated to Dr. Lawrence Atingdui, a Ghanaian scholar who joined our project with great enthusiasm and worked on it with unbelievable energy and dedication, despite a serious heart condition, until his untimely death in September of 1993. In his devotion to knowledge, his drive for objectivity and precision, and his warm and open spirit, Lawrence Atingdui personified the qualities that all of us involved in this project hope will always guide research in this new field, and that we hope have guided this project throughout.

Lester M. Salamon
Helmut K. Anheier
Baltimore, Maryland, U.S.A.

SUMMARY OF PRINCIPAL
FINDINGS

Background

Changing social and economic realities coupled with declining confidence in the capabilities of government have recently placed new demands on the thousands of private social service agencies, hospitals, health clinics, schools, universities, day care centers, development organizations, environmental groups, and others that comprise the private nonprofit, or voluntary, sector throughout the world. However, far too little is known in solid empirical terms about the scope or structure of this sector, or about its ability to respond to these new demands.

To remedy this, an international team of researchers working under the auspices of the Johns Hopkins University Institute for Policy Studies in the United States launched a major project to analyze the scope, structure, financing, and role of the private, nonprofit sector in 12 countries (the U.S., the U.K., France, Germany, Italy, Hungary, Japan, Brazil, Ghana, Egypt, Thailand, and India) using a common framework and approach. Detailed empirical data were assembled particularly on the first seven of these countries. The major findings are as follows:

Scope and scale

1. The nonprofit sector embraces a vast collection of organizations that share five common features. They are: (a) formally constituted; (b) organizationally separate from government; (c)

non-profit-seeking; (d) self-governing; and (e) voluntary to some significant degree. For the purposes of this project, two further restrictions were introduced to limit attention to organizations that are also: (f) nonreligious; and (g) nonpolitical.

2. The nonprofit sector, so defined, is a major economic force, employing 11.8 million workers in the seven countries for which complete empirical data were compiled. It thus accounts for one out of every 20 jobs, and one out of every 8 service jobs.

3. Employment in the nonprofit sector in these countries exceeds the combined employment of the largest private company in each country (General Motors, Hitachi, Alcatel-Alsthom, Daimler-Benz, Fiat, and Unilever) by a factor of 6 to 1.

4. In addition to the 11.8 million paid employees, the nonprofit sector makes use of volunteer labor that is the equivalent of another 4.7 million full-time workers.

5. At $604.3 billion (474.7 billion ECU), the operating expenditures of the nonprofit sector in these 7 countries represents the equivalent of 4.5 percent of the gross domestic product of the countries, and 4 times the gross sales of General Motors, the world's largest private corporation.

6. The nonprofit sector is not only large, but also growing. Indeed, in three countries for which historical data could be assembled (France, Germany, and the U.S.), the nonprofit sector accounted for 13 percent of the net new jobs added between 1980 and 1990.

Variations among countries

7. The United States has the largest nonprofit sector in both absolute and relative terms, with 6.9 percent of total employment.

8. France, Germany, and the U.K. all have roughly comparable, and quite sizable, nonprofit sectors despite significant disparities in legal traditions, government structures, and levels of reliance

on the state for social welfare. In each of these countries, the nonprofit sector accounts for 3–4 percent of all jobs and 9–10 percent of all employment in the service sector.

9. Though virtually nonexistent five years ago, the nonprofit sector in Hungary already boasts over 20,000 organizations and accounts for 3.2 percent of all service jobs.

10. Though smaller in relative terms than its counterparts elsewhere, the Japanese nonprofit sector is the second largest in absolute terms, employing more people than its counterparts in Germany, France, and the United Kingdom.

11. The number of nonprofit organizations is nearly 20,000 in Egypt and close to 200,000 in Brazil. The Thai nonprofit sector includes over 15,000 registered organizations and countless unregistered village and community associations.

Composition

12. An average of three-fourths of all nonprofit expenditures fall into four major fields: education and research, health, social services, and culture and recreation. However, the exact proportions in these fields differ from country to country.

13. In Japan and the U.K., the dominant field of nonprofit activity is education. In Germany and the U.S., it is health. In France and Italy it is social services. In Hungary it is culture and recreation. And in the developing countries, it is development, broadly defined.

Revenue

14. Only 10 percent of nonprofit revenue on average comes from private giving. Even in the United States, private giving accounts for less than 20 percent of nonprofit revenues.

15. The largest single source of nonprofit revenue, on average, is private fees and sales followed by public sector support. Private

fees and sales account, on average, for 47 percent of nonprofit income and public sector support for 43 percent.

16. In two countries—Germany and France—government is the dominant source of nonprofit income, reflecting a substantial collaboration between the nonprofit sector and the state. In virtually all countries, however, the public sector is a major source of nonprofit finance.

17. Private fee and sales income is particularly important in financing nonprofit business, cultural and recreational, education, housing, and environmental organizations.

18. Government support is particularly important in financing nonprofit health, social service, and advocacy organizations.

Implications

19. Given the growing scope and importance of the nonprofit sector on the world scene, a number of key issues will need to be addressed in the years ahead, including: (i) improving the sector's visibility and base of knowledge; (ii) ensuring a more open and supportive legal environment; (iii) developing effective partnerships with government; (iv) expanding private charitable support; (v) ensuring accountability; (vi) improving training; and (vii) coming to terms with globalization.

ABOUT THE AUTHORS

Lester M. Salamon is a full professor at The Johns Hopkins University and the director of the Johns Hopkins Institute for Policy Studies and the Johns Hopkins Comparative Nonprofit Sector Project. Prior to this he served as Deputy Associate Director of the U.S. Office of Management and Budget, and as director of the Center for Governance and Management Research and of the Nonprofit Sector Project at The Urban Institute in Washington, D.C.

Dr. Salamon is the author of over 100 books, monographs, and articles on alternative instruments of government action, social welfare and urban development policy, and the scope, structure, and role of the private nonprofit sector in the United States and elsewhere in the world. Dr. Salamon's most recent books include *Partners in Public Service: Government-Nonprofit Relations in the Modern Welfare State* (Johns Hopkins University Press, 1994); *America's Nonprofit Sector: A Primer* (The Foundation Center, 1992); *Government and the Third Sector: Emerging Relationships in Welfare States* (edited with Benjamin Gidron and Ralph Kramer) (Jossey-Bass, 1992); *Human Capital and America's Future: An Economic Strategy for the 90s* (Johns Hopkins University Press, 1991); *Beyond Privatization: The Tools of Government Action* (The Urban Institute Press, 1989); and *The Federal Budget and the Nonprofit Sector* (The Urban Institute Press, 1982).

Dr. Salamon is past vice-chair of the International Society for Third-Sector Research (ISTR) and is an Associate Editor of *Voluntas* and *Nonprofit and Voluntary Sector Quarterly*. He received his

B.A. in Economics and Policy Studies from Princeton University and his Ph.D. in Government from Harvard University.

Helmut K. Anheier is an Associate Professor of Sociology at Rutgers University, and a senior research associate at the Johns Hopkins Institute for Policy Studies. Prior to this, he was Social Affairs Officer at the United Nations' International Narcotics Control Board, and held research appointments at the Program on Nonprofit Organizations, Yale University, and the University of Cologne, Germany.

Dr. Anheier is founding co-editor of *Voluntas*, the international journal of research on nonprofit organizations. His recent publications include *The Third Sector: Comparative Studies of Nonprofit Organizations* (DeGruyter, 1990), as well as numerous articles that have appeared in journals such as *American Journal of Sociology, Social Forces, Annual Review of Sociology, Contemporary Sociology, Sociological Forum, International Sociology, World Development, Annals of Public and Cooperative Economics, Voluntas, Nonprofit and Voluntary Sector Quarterly, Nonprofit Management and Leadership, Urban Affairs Quarterly, Zeitschrift für Soziologie, Journal für Sozialforschung, Revue des Etudes Coopératives, Mutualistes et Associatives* and *Economistas*.

Dr. Anheier graduated from the University of Trier, Germany, in 1980, and holds a Ph.D. in sociology from Yale University. He is founding board member of the International Society for Third-Sector Research, and member of the Editorial Board of several social science journals.

Chapter 1

INTRODUCTION

A major reappraisal of the role of the state is currently under way throughout the world—in the developed countries of North America, Europe, and Asia; in the developing societies of Asia, Africa, and Latin America; and in the former Soviet bloc. Prompted by dissatisfaction with the cost and effectiveness of exclusive reliance on government to address the social welfare and developmental challenges of our time, efforts have been launched to find alternative ways to respond.[1]

A new paradigm?

Whatever its merits or demerits, this reevaluation of the role of the state has usefully called into question not only our existing policies, but the very way we organize our thinking about the structure of social and economic life.

Despite the immense diversity of organizations that comprise modern society, we have come to accept the existence of two grand complexes of institutions—two broad sectors—into which it has become conventional to divide social life. We refer to these typically as the *market* and the *state*, or the *private* and the *public* sectors. Notwithstanding the tremendous variety of actual institutional types to which the abstract concepts of the market and the state refer—ranging from corner groceries to gigantic multinational corporations and from tribal councils to complex governmental bureaucracies—these abstractions have come to command acceptance as meaningful, indeed necessary, analytical

1

constructs without which it is impossible to understand or describe our institutional existence. "Market" and "state" have become what the sociologist Eviatar Zerubavel calls "islands of meaning," cognitive devices that group together objects to facilitate recognition and communication.[2] Not only have we come to consider the marker and the state as such "islands of meaning" in our conceptual maps of social and economic life, we have come to consider them the *only* such islands and have organized our economic reporting systems and our public policies accordingly.

What recent dissatisfaction with the role of the state has done, however, is to challenge this two-sector conceptualization rather fundamentally. It has done so by focusing attention on a third set of institutions that has long made major contributions to the alleviation of human problems throughout the world, but that has been largely overlooked in both scholarly inquiry and public debates: a set of organizations that are private in form but public in purpose.

Such organizations have been called on recently to substitute for government social welfare spending in the United States and the United Kingdom, to help overcome the exclusion of the poor in France, to promote pluralism in Sweden, and to help foster a "civil society" in Russia and Central Europe.[3] In the developing world as well, such nongovernmental, but not-for-profit, institutions have come to be seen as crucial catalysts for a new approach to development stressing grass-roots involvement and "assisted self-reliance."[4] In its May 1986 statement to the Special Session of the United Nations General Assembly on Africa's Economic and Social Crisis, for example, the Council of Ministers of the Organization of African Unity and the Conference of Ministers of the Economic Commission for Africa thus challenged the long-standing assumption that state action alone can ensure African survival and development and called instead for the creation of a more "enabling environment" for private action, both nonprofit and for-profit.[5]

While it is not quite fair to suggest that policymakers have begun looking to such private, not-for-profit organizations as *the* cure for the perceived crises of socialism, development, and the welfare state, it is certainly the case that they are being called on to play a much larger role than in the recent past in virtually every part of the world. In the process, a "third sector" outside the market and the state has increasingly come into view as a crucial actor in modern social and economic life.

The problem

The problem, however, is that the increased expectations now being directed to this "third sector" are not based on a very clear understanding of the nature of this sector or what its capabilities really are. Indeed, there is little agreement even about the existence, let alone the precise contours, of a definable "third sector" occupying a distinctive social space outside both the market and the state.

Conceptual confusion

One manifestation of this is the terminological confusion that prevails in the field. The German concept of *Verein*, the French *économie sociale*, the British *public charities*, the Japanese *kōeki hōjin*, the American *nonprofit sector*, the Central European *foundation*, and the Latin American and African *NGO or nongovernmental organization* are not simply linguistically different. They reflect wholly different concepts and refer to distinctly different groupings of institutions.[6] Thus, for example, the French "social economy" sector embraces both cooperatives and mutuals such as mutual banks and insurance companies that are not normally included as part of the "nonprofit sector" in the United States or "the voluntary sector" in the U.K. Even within the same country or language group a wide variety of different terms is used to depict the set of organizations of concern to us here, and each has its own nuance of meaning. Thus in the U.K., organizations outside the market and the state are variously referred to as "voluntary organizations," "public charities," "charitable organizations," and "informal organizations"—each one depicting a slightly different set of actual organizations.

Gross lack of information

Not surprisingly, given this conceptual confusion, even the most basic features of this sector—its size, internal structure, financing, and relations with other sectors—are not known in a solid, empirical way for more than one or two countries, and even then only imperfectly. As a consequence, it is difficult for policymakers and the general public to understand the role that these organizations really play or to comprehend the contribution they can, or should, make to public life. Worse yet, perceptions of the sector are too often clouded by a variety of myths, some of them ideologically based, that distort the prevailing realities, confuse efforts at understanding, and often lead to misguided policies. Politicians on both the political Left and the political Right have had reason to downplay the role of these organizations or otherwise discredit their contribution to modern life—the former as part of the effort to build a case for state action in the social realm, and the latter to justify attacks on the state as the destroyer of intermediate groups. The upshot has been to remove the "third sector" from our conceptual screens even as it continued to grow and prosper.

Misleading data

Beyond this, what data do exist on this set of organizations have often been grossly misleading. Government statistical offices rarely gather data on the nonprofit sector, and when they do, they often do not report it separately. The only data regularly available on the nonprofit sector in the United States until the late 1970s, for example, was a data series on private, philanthropic giving.[7] The impression was widespread, therefore, that the scale of the nonprofit sector was roughly equal to the scale of private giving. Not until 1981, with the publication by the Census Bureau of a separate survey of tax-exempt service industries, did it become clear that private giving was only a fraction of the revenue of the nonprofit sector, and a surprisingly small one at that.[8] Even so, this survey itself reported only on aggregate expenditures, number of establishments, and number of employees, but gave no information on revenues.[9]

In other countries the situation, if anything, is often worse. Even when data exist for individual subsectors in particular countries, they are often based on definitions that make them incomparable to similar data in other countries. Thus, because they include information on mutual banks and insurance companies, data on the French "social economy" sector cannot easily be compared to data on the U.S., German, or Italian nonprofit sectors. Efforts to compare the levels of government support to the nonprofit sector in the United States and the United Kingdom are regularly thrown into chaos by the inclusion of in-kind voucher payments in the U.S. and their exclusion from government data on "grants" to the voluntary sector in the U.K., and by the frequent tendency of U.K. analysts to exclude payments through "quangos," or quasi-nongovernmental organizations.

How serious the data situation with regard to the nonprofit sector is at the international level is most clearly apparent in the most comprehensive reporting system on national economies worldwide, the United Nations System of National Accounts. This system was explicitly designed to inject a degree of uniformity into economic reporting among at least the major industrial countries. While it has made impressive headway overall, however, the system has yet to deal effectively with the nonprofit sector. In the first place, the U.N. System of Accounts treats the nonprofit sector as a residual.[10] Thus, any organization that receives half or more of its income from government is classified as a government agency by the U.N. system, and any agency that receives half or more of its income from fees and service charges is classified as a private business. Using this definition, most of the U.K., German, and U.S. nonprofit sectors would be defined out of existence.

Perhaps not surprisingly, therefore, the U.N. national account data contain precious little information on the nonprofit sector, and much of what is included is grossly misleading. Thus, of a total of 168 countries, only 30 report data on the nonprofit sector at all, and only two provide the United Nations Statistical Office with a complete set of the information called for on this sector.[11] Reports drawing on these data therefore present a picture of the nonprofit sector that could best be described as bizarre. Thus, according to the most recent Organization for Economic Cooperation and Development (OECD) compilation, the nonprofit sector in France accounted for a minuscule three-tenths of 1 percent (0.26 percent) of gross domestic product, one-ninth the size of its counterpart in Germany (see Figure 1.1).[12] In only one country (the U.S.) did the nonprofit sector account for as much as 3 percent of gross domestic product according to these data.

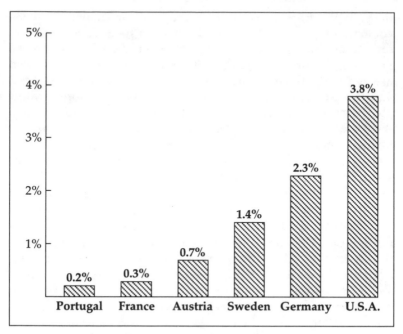

Figure 1.1   Nonprofit size according to OECD, 1991 (Value added as % of GDP)

Source: OECD, National Accounts, Detailed Tables, 1976–1988 (Paris: OECD 1991)

More recently, the European Statistical Office, in an effort to plug this glaring gap in basic data on an increasingly crucial segment of the European economy, prepared its own estimates of the size of the European "not-for-profit sector." But if the OECD erred on the side of exclusion, Eurostat erred on the side of inclusion, giving national statistical offices carte blanche to include all manner of entities and all types of transactions. Thus some countries covered cooperatives along with large mutual insurance companies and voluntary associations; others excluded the latter and focused primarily on cooperatives; still others excluded cooperatives but included building societies and pension funds. Adding further to the confusion, the turnover of cooperatives is added in some countries to the premiums charged by insurance companies, the expenditures of voluntary associations, and even the assets reported by cooperative banks, life insurance companies, and pension funds. Instead of the 0.26 percent of GDP reported by OECD in 1991, therefore, the Eurostat data suggest that the French nonprofit sector as of 1993 accounted for an astounding 49.3 percent of the French economy, just slightly ahead of Germany's 42.6 percent![13] Clearly, when estimates issued by reputable research organizations within three years of each other are off by a factor of almost 200 to 1, it is a sign that something serious is awry in the measurement and conceptualization of a social phenomenon.

Summary

In short, at a time of growing awareness of a "third sector" of private institutions serving essentially public purposes that is being called on increasingly to handle a host of social functions—from community care to the promotion of economic development, from housing to environmental clean-up—basic information about the nature, scope, structure, and financing of the institutions that comprise this sector internationally remains abysmally inadequate. Under the circumstances, improvement in basic knowledge about this set of organizations has become a matter of urgent practical, and not just academic, concern.

The Johns Hopkins Comparative Nonprofit Sector Project

It was in response to this concern that a group of international philanthropic leaders meeting in Bonn, Germany, in 1988 concluded that a systematic effort was needed to put the "nonprofit" or "voluntary" sector permanently on the economic map of the world. Out of this consensus grew the Johns Hopkins Comparative Nonprofit Sector Project, the first worldwide effort to chart the scope, structure, role, and operations of the nonprofit sector at the international level using a consciously comparative approach.

Objectives

Launched in May 1990, the Johns Hopkins Comparative Nonprofit Sector Project is essentially a collaborative effort on the part of

7

researchers in a dozen countries throughout the world to document some of the key features of the private nonprofit or voluntary sector in their respective countries using a common framework and approach. More specifically, this project was designed to accomplish five major objectives:

1) To clarify the scope, structure, and financial base of the nonprofit sector in a cross-section of countries using a coherent, comparative approach;

2) To understand the historic roots and legal position of the nonprofit sector in different parts of the world, and the factors that promote or retard the sector's development;

3) To provide a better foundation for public and private policies toward the nonprofit sector;

4) To improve awareness of this sector on the part of government and private leaders and the general public; and

5) To foster local capacity to carry this work forward in the future.

Approach

To pursue these objectives, we developed a project that has *six key characteristics*:

1) Empirical
A central goal of this project was to get beyond the impressionistic accounts that have characterized many of the prior discussions of the nonprofit sector in different countries. Accordingly, the project has sought to gather systematic empirical data in addition to other types of information. While such data do not exhaust the concerns of the project, they certainly give it a distinctive flavor.

2) Comparative
Numerous efforts have been made to assemble analyses of the nonprofit sector in different countries.[14] However, most of these either represent collections of works developed by individual scholars using their own methods, definitions, and approaches; or analyses of relatively narrow subsectors (e.g., education) rather than the nonprofit sector as a whole. The Johns Hopkins

Comparative Nonprofit Sector Project differs from these other efforts by pursuing a more explicitly comparative approach, focusing on a broad cross-section of countries, utilizing a common definition, and adhering to a unified methodology. While more complex, such an approach has considerable advantages over separate national efforts proceeding independently: it makes it possible to put national experiences into comparative perspective, to achieve greater clarity and reliability, to share information across national borders, to test alternative theories purporting to explain why the nonprofit sector prospers in some settings and not in others, and to achieve greater efficiency and cost-effectiveness by centralizing some of the core analytical tasks.

Selection Criteria. The key to this comparative approach was the selection of a reasonable cross-section of countries. Three criteria entered into this selection process.

The first was *theoretical relevance.* Prior research suggests a variety of factors that seem to encourage or retard the development of the nonprofit sector. In order to assess these theories in the light of the data we were developing, we sought to include countries that vary significantly in terms of these factors. In particular, according to this prior work, five sets of factors seem to be especially important in shaping the scope and scale of the nonprofit sector in a country:

- *Heterogeneity.* According to one well-known theory, the existence of the nonprofit sector is a result of inherent limitations of both the market and the state in providing "collective goods," i.e., goods like safe streets that, once produced, are available to everyone regardless of whether they have paid for them. Because of their collective nature, such goods are generally underproduced by the market system (if people can have these goods for free, no one will voluntarily choose to pay for them). According to classical economic theory, the existence of such collective goods explains why government is needed in a market economy. However, the more diverse the population, the more difficult it is for people to agree on what collective goods they should supply through the state. The result will be unsatisfied demand for collective goods on the part of different segments of the population. The function of the nonprofit sector, according to this theory, is to meet this unsatisfied demand for collective goods. The greater the diversity of the

9

population, therefore, the greater should be the size of the nonprofit sector.[15]

- *Scope of the welfare state.* If the size of the nonprofit sector should vary directly with the degree of heterogeneity of the population, according to this set of theories, it should also vary inversely with the scope of government social welfare protections. This is so, according to these theories, because the more citizens provide for themselves through government, the less is left for the nonprofit sector to do. According to this "gap-filling" theory, the greater the scope of the welfare state in a particular country, the smaller should be the nonprofit sector.
- *Level of development.* Another factor likely to affect the scale of the nonprofit sector is the level of economic development in a country. The impact of this factor is very complex and not well understood, however. On the one hand, many traditional societies have rich tapestries of nongovernmental/noncommercial organizations that bear striking resemblance to "third sector" organizations.[16] Such organizations are engaged in mutual aid, alleviation of poverty, and economic development. At the same time, modern nonprofit organizations seem to depend heavily on the emergence of a relatively independent commercial or professional middle class which requires a reasonable level of development. For this reason, the scale of nonprofit activity may be retarded in developing countries. Under any circumstances, the interplay between traditional mutual aid organizations and modern nonprofit organizations adds a special twist to the dynamics of third-sector operation in less developed countries.
- *Legal framework.* A fourth factor thought to affect the scope of the nonprofit sector in a country is the legal framework that exists. Generally speaking, common law legal systems seem to provide a more supportive environment for the emergence of nonprofit organizations than do civil law systems.[17] This is so because such systems assume an inherent right on the part of citizens to form private associations whereas in civil law systems different institutional forms must be explicitly provided for in law before they can legitimately exist, and even then often require state approval to function.
- *Historical traditions.* Finally, various historical and religious traditions can encourage or discourage the formation of nonprofit

organizations. For example, the Jacobin tradition in France, with its emphasis on the role of the state as the embodiment of the "general will," has provided a significant barrier to the formation of associations. On the other hand, in Germany, a strong tradition of "subsidiarity" growing out of Catholic social thought has offered a quite hospitable clime for the growth of nonprofit institutions. More generally, the Judeo-Christian tradition is thought to promote charity and voluntary action in ways that may be less pronounced in other traditions. In a sense, each society thus has its own organizational "template," its own traditions for organizing social and economic life. A clear understanding of the nonprofit sector must therefore embrace a sufficient range of such organizational and religious traditions.

In addition to these theoretical considerations, a second factor affecting our choice of countries was *manageability*. In view of the pioneering nature of this work, it was necessary to keep the number of countries limited in order to make the effort manageable and ensure consistency in the results.

Finally, our choice of sites was also affected by considerations of *practical feasibility*. This included the prospects for finding local financial support for the project, and the likelihood of identifying a qualified local associate to carry out the local data gathering and analysis.

Country selection. Using these criteria, we identified 12 countries for initial inclusion in the project. They included six developed countries (the U.S., the U.K., France, Germany, Italy, and Japan), five developing countries (Brazil, Ghana, Egypt, Thailand, and India), and one former Communist bloc country (Hungary).[18]

As reflected in Table 1.1, the six developed countries were chosen to reflect different levels of reliance on the state in the provision of social welfare benefits. Thus France, a unitary civil law country, is a highly developed modern welfare state, with close to 30 percent of its gross domestic product devoted to government social welfare spending. At the opposite extreme, the U.S. and Japan devote less than 13 percent of their gross domestic products to government social welfare spending. However, these countries differ along other dimensions. Thus the U.S. is a highly decentralized common law country with a federal political system and a high level of population heterogeneity.

Table 1.1

Project sites

TYPE	Government social welfare spending				
	LOW	MEDIUM		HIGH	
DEVELOPED	Japan (12%) U.S.A. (13%)	U.K. (20%) Germany (23%) Italy (23%)		France (29%)	
DEVELOPING	South America	Africa	Middle East	South Asia	South East Asia
	Brazil	Ghana	Egypt	India	Thailand
FORMER SOCIALIST BLOC	Hungary				

Japan is a centralized, civil law country with little heterogeneity but a tradition of reliance on private corporations for social welfare protections. In between are Germany, Italy, and the U.K., which devote 20–23 percent of their GDP to government social welfare spending, but which have traditions that provide opportunities for nonprofit action—the common law tradition in the U.K., the tradition of subsidiarity in Germany, and the regional diversity and strong tradition of Church involvement in social welfare in Italy. (For further detail on the characteristics of the project countries, see Appendix A.)

The choice of the five developing countries was designed to include a major country embracing each of the major geographical regions of the world, and each of the major religious traditions—Brazil in South America, Ghana in Africa, Egypt in the Arab world, India on the Asian subcontinent, and Thailand in Southeast Asia. This was done to test the widespread belief that the nonprofit sector is essentially a Western phenomenon.

Finally, in Eastern Europe, Hungary was selected because of the early emergence of nonprofit institutions there.

Although more countries might usefully have been included in this project, 12 was the maximum we considered to be manageable given our stress on comparative data assembly and analysis. Even so, the countries included provide an extraordinary range of experiences with nonprofit institutions, creating a strong basis

Table 1.2

Defining features of the nonprofit sector

General:
• Formal organizations
• Private
• Non-profit-distributing / non-commercial
• Self-governing
• Voluntary
This project only:
• Nonreligious
• Nonpolitical

for comparing nonprofit development in both advanced and less advanced societies, representing all the major religious traditions and regions of the world, and in contexts that differ widely in their reliance on nonprofit organizations and the state and in their basic legal structures.

Because of limitations of data and resources, it was not possible to assemble complete empirical data on the five developing countries. Much of the empirical data presented in this report, therefore, focuses on the remaining seven countries (France, Germany, Hungary, Italy, Japan, U.K., and U.S.). The inclusion of the five developing countries nevertheless enriches the discussion throughout, and in Chapter 6 we examine these countries explicitly.

3) Common definition

In order to make systematic data gathering possible in these 12 countries, it was necessary to develop a common definition of the nonprofit sector to establish the boundaries of the sector for the purpose of this project. This was done by soliciting from a team of field associates an analysis of the different terms used in the various project countries to depict this set of organizations and the types of organizations to which the different terms apply. By overlaying these different terms and concepts, it was possible to identify certain key features that all organizations considered to be part of the "nonprofit sector" share in virtually all countries. Five such features in particular were identified. What is more, to keep the scope of the project within manageable limits, we added two further restrictions to exclude organizations that, while formally within the sector as we defined it, nevertheless lay outside our principal area of interest.[19]

The result was a set of seven factors that defined the organizations of interest to us in this project. To be covered by the project, therefore, an organization had to be:

- *Formal*, i.e., institutionalized to some extent. What is important is that the organization have some institutional reality to it. In some countries this is signified by a formal charter of incorporation. But institutional reality can also be demonstrated in other ways where legal incorporation is not readily available—by having regular meetings, officers, or rules of procedure, or some degree of organizational permanence. Purely ad hoc, informal, and temporary gatherings of people are not considered part of the nonprofit sector under this definition, even though they may be quite important in people's lives. Otherwise the concept of the nonprofit sector becomes far too amorphous and ephemeral to grasp and examine.
- *Private*, i.e., institutionally separate from government. Nonprofit organizations are neither part of the governmental apparatus nor governed by boards dominated by government officials. This does not mean that they may not receive significant government support or that government officials cannot sit on their boards. The key here is that nonprofit organizations are fundamentally private institutions in basic structure.
- *Non-profit-distributing*, i.e., not returning profits generated to their owners or directors. Nonprofit organizations may accumulate profits in a given year, but the profits must be plowed back into the basic mission of the agency, not distributed to the organizations' "owners" or governing board. In this sense, nonprofit organizations are private organizations that do not exist primarily to generate profits. Rather, they have some "public" purpose and are not primarily commercial in operation and purpose. This differentiates nonprofit organizations from the other component of the private sector—private businesses.
- *Self-governing*, i.e., equipped to control their own activities. Nonprofit organizations have their own internal procedures for governance and are not controlled by outside entities.
- *Voluntary*, i.e., involving some meaningful degree of voluntary participation, either in the actual conduct of the agency's

activities or in the management of its affairs. This does not mean that all or most of the income of an organization must come from voluntary contributions, or that most of its staff must be volunteers. The presence of some voluntary input, even if only a voluntary board of directors, suffices to qualify an organization as in some sense "voluntary."

- *Nonreligious,* i.e., not primarily involved in the promotion of religious worship or religious education. Religiously affiliated nonprofit service organizations are included in the project, but not the congregations, synagogues, mosques, or churches where religious worship takes place. Such religious institutions are properly part of the nonprofit sector but were excluded from the analysis here to keep the project manageable.
- *Nonpolitical,* i.e., not primarily involved in promoting candidates for elected office. Organizations that engage in advocacy activity to change government policies on particular topics (e.g., civil rights, the environment) are included in the project, but political parties and other organizations devoted principally to getting people elected to public office are not. Here, again, such organizations are properly part of the nonprofit sector, but they were excluded from the analysis here to keep the effort manageable.

For the purposes of this project, therefore, only organizations that fit these seven criteria are included. Even so, this includes an immense variety of types of organizations. In particular, we developed a *classification system,* the *International Classification of Nonprofit Organizations (ICNPO),* to group these organizations systematically.[20] As reflected in Table 1.3, 10 broad categories of organizations are thus included within the project's terms of reference, ranging from cultural and recreational organizations through business and professional associations, and including educational institutions, health providers, social service agencies, environmental organizations, advocacy groups, and NGOs engaged in development work. (For a complete outline of the International Classification of Nonprofit Organizations, see Appendix B.) Not included, however, as shown in Table 1.4, are religious congregations, political parties, cooperatives, mutual savings banks, mutual insurance companies, and similar enterprises.

Although no single term adequately characterizes the various institutions that fit this "structural-operational" definition, we

Table 1.3

Types of nonprofit organizations covered

- Culture, recreation
- Education, research
- Health
- Social services
- Environment
- Development and housing
- Civic and advocacy
- Philanthropic intermediaries
- Business and professional
- Other

Table 1.4

Types of organizations excluded

- Religious congregations
- Political parties
- Cooperatives
- Mutual savings banks
- Mutual insurance companies
- Government agencies

will follow the convention set in the U.N. System of National Accounts and adopted by OECD and Eurostat in its European System of Accounts and refer to them as "nonprofit organizations," or the "nonprofit sector."

4) Common methodology
In addition to a common definition, the project utilized a common methodology and approach in developing its basic information. To help ensure this, a set of basic "field guides" was developed to structure the work on each topic covered in each country. More specifically, the project drew on the following major types of information in each country:
- *National income and subsector data systems.* A central premise of this project was that existing national income data systems and subsector surveys, at least in the advanced industrial societies, contain far more data on the nonprofit sector than is

commonly recognized. The problem, however, is that these data are buried in statistical series that rarely break out the nonprofit sector in published results, or that do so only partially. National income statistics in the U.K., Germany, the United States, France, and Japan, for example, regularly survey both for-profit and nonprofit "establishments" to determine employment levels and other basic economic parameters by "standard industrial classification."[21] By systematically assembling the results of these surveys, making various estimates to break out the nonprofit sector, and using best-available statistical methods to estimate key relationships (e.g., between numbers of employees, the total wage bill, and total expenditures), it was possible to assemble at least a rough estimate of the scope and scale of the nonprofit sector in each country, particularly with the aid of specialized surveys conducted on particular parts of the nonprofit sector by subsector organizations (eg., the American Hospital Association survey of hospitals in the United States or the survey of sports clubs by the German Sport Federation).[22] (For a more complete statement of the methodology used in the different countries, see Appendix C.) The base year used for this analysis throughout was 1990.

- *Targeted surveys.* Useful though existing national income data sources were, they inevitably left gaps in coverage of particular portions of the sector or particular aspects of it (e.g., funding sources) in particular countries. To cope with this problem, the project design included targeted surveys aimed at filling these gaps, at least on a partial basis. Such surveys were carried out in the U.K., Germany, Brazil, Thailand, Italy, and Hungary. Here, again, care was taken to utilize a common survey form wherever possible. In addition to the organizational surveys, surveys were also conducted of giving and volunteering patterns in Germany and France.
- *Literature review.* In addition to its assembly and analysis of statistical data, this project also relied heavily on existing literature on the history of social policy and the nonprofit sector, as well as on the legal treatment of nonprofit organizations in the target countries.
- *Interviews.* Finally, to determine the current status of the nonprofit sector, and of government policy toward it, in-depth

interviews were conducted with key informants in each target country.

5) *Collaborative: a team approach*

While being systematically comparative and using a common definition and approach, the project described here was also fundamentally collaborative, utilizing a team approach that included a small core staff and a network of local associates in the separate countries. The responsibility of the core staff was to formulate the basic project design, develop the basic information-gathering forms or "field guides," and monitor the work in the individual countries to ensure consistency in both quality and approach. The responsibility of the local associates was to conduct the actual data gathering, assembly, and analysis.

The local associates also played a critical role in the basic design of the project, however, including participation in the development of the basic project definition of the nonprofit sector, the classification scheme for differentiating nonprofit organizations, and the "field guides" used to gather common information in the separate countries. To help promote this collaborative approach, the entire project team met every eight to 12 months to develop basic analytical approaches, review progress, comment on project products, and compare notes on findings.

6) *Consultative*

Finally, to ensure that the project had the maximum input from experts in this field, both internationally and in the individual project countries, an elaborate consultative structure was also put in place. This involved two sets of consultative committees:

- *Local advisory committees* in most of the project countries. The goal of these advisory committees was to secure the input of a wider community of experts and practitioners, ensure a degree of acceptance of the basic approach and strategy on the part of key actors concerned with the evolution of the nonprofit sector, and help with the dissemination of project results in the target countries.
- *An International Advisory Committee* consisting of key leaders of the nonprofit sector at the international level. This committee was designed to assist the core project staff in the development of the project, to review the basic approach, and to assist

in the dissemination of project products. The International Advisory Committee generally met with the project team at the regular project team meetings throughout the life of the project.

Conclusions

The nonprofit sector has recently come to occupy a central place in the debate over the future of social welfare and development policy throughout the world. Sadly, however, what is known about this sector lags badly behind the demands for information being generated by the policy process. Under these circumstances, improving the base of knowledge about this sector in a systematic, comparative fashion has become a matter not only of great academic interest, but also of urgent policy concern.

The Johns Hopkins Comparative Nonprofit Sector Project was conceived to help meet this concern and fill this need. To be sure, this project will not be the last word on the scope, structure, and role of the nonprofit sector at the international level. Limitations of resources and data have inevitably necessitated compromises that we hope others will have the luxury to avoid. But whatever its limitations, this project nevertheless provides a first clear glimpse into a world that has been shrouded in fog for far too long, and a solid foundation on which others can build. In the chapters that follow we outline what this glimpse reveals.

Notes

1 For further detail on the set of social and economic forces accounting for the recent "global associational revolution," see Lester M. Salamon, "The Rise of the Nonprofit Sector," *Foreign Affairs*, Vol. 73, No. 4 (July/August 1994), pp. 111–124.
2 Eviatar Zerubavel, *The Fine Line* (Chicago: University of Chicago Press, 1991).
3 See, for example, Lester M. Salamon, "Rise of the Nonprofit Sector," 1994; Lester M. Salamon and Alan J. Abramson, *The Federal Budget and the Nonprofit Sector* (Washington, D.C.: The Urban Institute Press, 1982); Marilyn Taylor, "The Changing Role of the Nonprofit Sector in Britain: Moving Toward the Market," in

Benjamin Gidron, Ralph Kramer, and Lester M. Salamon, eds., *Government and the Nonprofit Sector: Emerging Relationships in Welfare States* (San Francisco: Jossey-Bass Publishers, 1992), pp. 147–175; B. Kouchner, ed., *Les nouvelles solidarités* (Paris: Presses Universitaires de France, 1990).

4 See, for example, Norman Uphoff, "Assisted Self-Reliance: Working With, Rather than for, the Poor," in John P. Lewis, ed., *Strengthening the Poor* (New Brunswick: Transaction Books, 1988), pp. 47–60. See also A. B. Durning, "Action at the Grass-roots: Fighting Poverty and Environmental Decline," *Worldwatch Paper*, No. 88 (Washington, D.C.: Worldwatch Institute, 1989); S. Annis, "Can Small-Scale Development Be a Large-Scale Policy? The Case of Latin America," *World Development*, Vol. 15, Supplement (August 1987), pp. 129–134; Anne Gordon Drabek, "Development Alternatives: The Challenge for NGOs," (*World Development*, Vol. 15 (1987)).

5 Aga Khan Foundation, "The Nairobi Statement," *Report of the Enabling Environment Conference: Effective Private Sector Contribution to Development in Sub-Saharan Africa*. Presented in Nairobi, Kenya, October 21–24, 1986 (Paris, 1987).

6 For a fuller description of these concepts and the meanings that lie behind them, see Lester M. Salamon and Helmut K. Anheier, eds., *Defining the Nonprofit Sector: A Cross-National Analysis* (Manchester: Manchester University Press, 1996).

7 This data series, reported in an annual report entitled *Giving USA*, is assembled by the American Association of Fund-Raising Counsel, Inc., a trade association representing private fund-raising firms.

8 One earlier estimate of the scale of the nonprofit sector was complied by Gabriel Rudney for the Commission on Private Philanthropy and Public Needs (the Filer Commission) in 1974. See Commission on Private Philanthropy and Public Needs, *Giving in America* (Washington, D.C.: U.S. Government Printing Office, 1975), p. 35.

9 U.S. Census Bureau, *1977 Census of Service Industries* (Washington, D.C.: U.S. Government Printing Office, 1981).

10 Helmut K. Anheier, Gabriel Rudney, and Lester M. Salamon, "The Nonprofit Sector and the United Nations System of Accounts: Country Applications of SNA Guidelines," *Voluntas*, Vol. 4, No. 4 (1993), pp. 486–501.

11 United Nations Statistical Office, *National Accounts Statistics: Main Aggregates and Detailed Tables 1988* (New York: United Nations, 1990).

12 Organization of Economic Cooperation and Development (OECD), *National Accounts, Detailed Tables, 1976–1988* (Paris: OECD, 1991), Table 9. Unless otherwise indicated, throughout this report, data on Germany refer to West Germany.

13 Eurostat, "A statistical profile of the cooperative, mutual and nonprofit sector and its organizations in the European Community," *Services and Transport*, Theme 7, Series B, Short-term trends. Supplement 2, 1993. One substantive difference between the OECD and Eurostat data is that the UN/OECD data report *"value added"* by the nonprofit sector as a percent of gross domestic product, whereas Eurostat records *"total expenditures"* as a share of gross domestic product. Since "value added" is a more narrow concept (roughly equivalent to wages for the nonprofit sector), we would expect it to be smaller. However, the sharp difference between OECD and Eurostat estimates cannot be accounted for by this technical difference alone.

14 See, for example, Estelle James, "The Nonprofit Sector in Comparative Perspective," in Walter W. Powell, ed., *The Nonprofit Sector: A Research Handbook* (New Haven: Yale University Press, 1987); Estelle James, ed., *The Nonprofit Sector in International Perspective: Studies in Comparative Culture and Policy* (Oxford: Oxford University Press, 1989); Helmut K. Anheier and Wolfgang Seibel, eds., *The Third Sector: Comparative Studies of Nonprofit Organizations* (Berlin: DeGruyter Publications, 1990); Kathleen McCarthy, Virginia Hodgkinson, and Russy Sumariwalla, eds., *The Nonprofit Sector in the Global Community* (San Francisco: Jossey-Bass Publishers, 1992); Benjamin Gidron, Ralph Kramer, and Lester M. Salamon, eds., *Government and the Third Sector: Emerging Relationships in Welfare States* (San Francisco: Jossey-Bass Publishers, 1992).

15 Burton Weisbrod, *The Voluntary Nonprofit Sector* (Lexington, Mass.: Lexington Books, 1978).

16 See, for example, Michael Bratton, "Beyond the State: Civil Society and Associational Life in Africa," *World Politics* (April 1989), pp. 407–430.

17 For further detail on this line of argument, see Lester M. Salamon and Helmut K. Anheier, "Caring Sector or Caring Society? Discovering the Nonprofit Sector Cross-Nationally," in Paul Schervisch, Virginia Hodgkinson, and Margaret Gates, eds., *Care and Community in Modern Society* (San Francisco: Jossey-Bass Publishers, 1995).

18 A thirteenth country, Sweden, was added after the project was under way, but is not included in the data reported here.

19 For a more complete statement of the considerations that went into the choice of definition of the nonprofit sector for the purposes of this project, see Lester M. Salamon and Helmut K. Anheier, "In Search of the Nonprofit Sector I: The Question of Definitions," *Voluntas*, Vol. 3, No. 2 (1992), pp. 125–151.

20 See Lester M. Salamon and Helmut K. Anheier, "In Search of the

Nonprofit Sector II: The Problem of Classification," *Voluntas*, Vol. 3, No. 2 (1992), pp. 267–309.

21 The Standard Industrial Classification (SIC) system essentially groups all economic activity into a number of basic "industries" and "sub-industries." SIC codes cover almost all of the activities in which the nonprofit sector is typically engaged, although the level of detail is not sufficiently fine in all industries to do justice to the nonprofit sector. Under the U.N. national system of accounts, most advanced industrial countries have incorporated the basic SIC system into their national income statistical systems. The classification system we have developed for the nonprofit sector is designed to fit squarely into this SIC system.

22 Similar work was carried out in the United States in the early 1980s and has been replicated several times since then. See Virginia Hodgkinson and Murray Weitzman, *Dimensions of the Independent Sector*, 3rd Edition (Washington, D.C.: Independent Sector, 1984); Gabriel Rudney and Murray S. Weitzman, "Significance of Employment and Earnings Trends in the Philanthropic Sector," *PONPO Working Paper* (New Haven: Program on Nonprofit Organizations, 1983).

Chapter 2

AN ECONOMIC FORCE

The dominant leitmotif of the 20th century has been the growth of the modern state. From the time that German Chancellor Otto von Bismarck redefined the role of the state to include the protection of worker welfare in the late 19th century, political debate in much of the Western world, and increasingly in the non-Western world as well, has focused on the steady expansion of state protections against the social and economic misfortunes that have accompanied the urbanization and industrialization of modern society.

Not surprisingly, given this dominant theme, the possibility that private, voluntary organizations might continue to play a major role in the face of an expanding welfare state has attracted little serious attention except among fringe conservative thinkers longing for a return to the good old days of individual initiative and wholly voluntary effort. In most advanced countries, the nonprofit sector is not only assumed not to be needed; it is assumed to have passed from the scene.

In fact, however, assertions about the demise of the nonprofit sector deserve the same response that American humorist Mark Twain gave to rumors about his untimely death. "These reports," remarked Twain, "have been greatly exaggerated."

In point of fact, the nonprofit sector remains a major presence in virtually every country of the world. Whether measured by what it does, or in more traditional economic terms, this set of institutions is a major force in our social and economic life.

Table 2.1

Nonprofit services

Country indicator	Nonprofit share (%)
Germany	
Hospital patient days	40
Residential care facilities	60
Day care slots	33
France	
Elementary and secondary students	20
Residential care residents	55
U.S.	
Hospital beds	51
Colleges, universities	49
Orchestras	95
Japan	
University students	77
Hospital patient days	40
Italy	
Residential care facilities	41
Kindergartens	21
U.K.	
Elementary and secondary students	22
Higher education institutions	100

Source: Johns Hopkins Comparative Nonprofit Sector Project

Outputs

Consider only the following salient facts:
• *In Germany,* as shown in Table 2.1—
-Four out of every 10 patient days in hospitals are spent in nonprofit institutions;
-Half of all nursing home residents are in nonprofit homes;
-60 percent of residential care facilities are nonprofit;
-One-third of all children in day care attend nonprofit facilities.
• *In France*—
-55 percent of residential care residents are in nonprofit homes;
-4 out of every 5 sports enthusiasts belong to nonprofit sports clubs;
-Almost 1 out of every 5 primary and secondary students are in nonprofit schools.
• *In the U.S.*—

-Over half of all hospital beds are in nonprofit hospitals;
-Half of all colleges and universities are nonprofit institutions;
-95 percent of all orchestras are nonprofit organizations;
-60 percent of all social service agencies are nonprofit.

- *In Japan—*
-Over 75 percent of all university students attend nonprofit institutions;
-Over 40 percent of hospital patient days are in nonprofit hospitals.

- *In the U.K.—*
-22 percent of students in primary and elementary schools are in nonprofit institutions;
-10 percent of dwelling units are built or rehabilitated by nonprofit organizations.

- *In Italy—*
-21 percent of kindergartens are nonprofit;
-41 percent of residential care facilities are nonprofit.

Employment

Behind these output measures lies a set of organizations of immense scale and scope. Though operating in significant part outside the market economy, these organizations are also important even in economic terms.

One measure of this is employment. To be sure, employment is an imperfect measure of the economic impact of the nonprofit sector since it ignores the important input of voluntary labor that these organizations also have available to them. If anything, therefore, employment probably *understates* the real economic value of the nonprofit sector.

Even after taking this into account, however, employment in the nonprofit sector is quite substantial. In particular, in the seven major countries for which we collected complete empirical data (the U.S., the U.K., France, Germany, Italy, Hungary, and Japan), the nonprofit sector as of 1990 employed the equivalent of 11.8 million full-time workers, as shown in Table 2.2. This represents close to one out of every 20 workers in these countries. And if we focus just on the service sector, which is where the nonprofit sector operates, the picture is even more impressive. Altogether,

Table 2.2

Nonprofit employment: seven countries

Indicator	Amount
Total nonprofit employees	11,786,620
Nonprofit employment as % of	
Total employment	4.5
Service employment	11.8
Government employment	27.7

Source: Johns Hopkins Comparative Nonprofit Sector Project

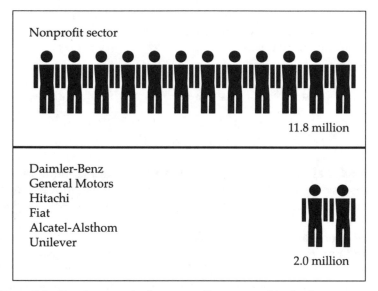

Figure 2.1 Employment in the nonprofit sector and in the largest corporations in seven countries

the nonprofit sector in these seven countries accounts for one out of every eight service sector jobs.

Put somewhat differently, as reflected in Figure 2.1, if we were to add together the total employment of the largest private business firms in the six developed market economies—General Motors in the U.S., Daimler-Benz in Germany, Alcatel-Alsthom in France, Fiat in Italy, Hitachi in Japan, and Unilever in the U.K.—we would end up with only one-sixth as many full-time

Table 2.3

Nonprofit expenditures: seven countries

Operating expenditures, 1990
• 474.7 billion ECU
• 604.3 billion US$
• 4.5 percent of combined GDP

Source: Johns Hopkins Comparative Nonprofit Sector Project

equivalent workers as are employed in the private, nonprofit sector in these countries. In other words, nonprofit employment in these countries is six times larger than employment in these large private companies.

Expenditures

Employment, of course, is only one way to measure the economic importance of the nonprofit sector. Equally relevant is the level of annual operating expenditures. Operating expenditures refer to the amounts organizations spend for annual operations. They exclude expenditures for capital items such as buildings or machinery that last more than a single year. Operating expenditures thus provide an excellent measure of an organization's annual economic activity.

Operating expenditures, of course, are not a perfect measure of the economic impact of the nonprofit sector for the reason noted above: in addition to their paid employment, these organizations employ numerous volunteers who contribute to agency activity yet do not show up in operating expenditures. Even with such volunteer input excluded, however, the nonprofit sector turns out to be a gigantic economic presence.

Thus, in the seven countries for which we were able to assemble complete operating expenditure data, the nonprofit sector, as we have defined it, had expenditures in 1990 of 474.7 billion ECU, or 604.3 billion US$. This sector thus represented 4.5 percent of the combined gross domestic product of these countries (see Table 2.3).[1] To put this into context, General Motors, the world's largest private corporation, had sales in 1990 of $132.4

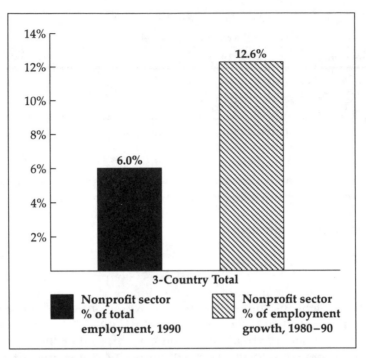

Figure 2.2   Nonprofit contribution to employment growth, 1980–1990, U.S., Germany, France

billion, or less than one-fourth as great as that of the nonprofit sector in these seven countries.

Employment growth

Not only is the nonprofit sector in these seven countries an immense economic presence, but it has also been a growing presence, particularly in recent years. In fact, it has been a more potent source of job growth than other segments of the economy. To see this, we compared the nonprofit share of total employment to the nonprofit share of job *growth* during the decade of the 1980s for three countries for which historical data could be assembled (U.S., France, and Germany). The results, reflected in Figure 2.2, are quite striking. With about 6 percent of total employment as of 1990, nonprofit organizations accounted for nearly 13 percent of the net new jobs added in these countries between 1980 and 1990. In other words, the nonprofit sector was proportionately almost twice as successful in adding new jobs during this period as its overall scale would suggest. What is more, this was not simply a product of the performance of just one of the countries. As Chapter 3 will show in more detail, for all three countries examined, the nonprofit contribution to job *growth* outdistanced the overall nonprofit share of total jobs, indicating that this sector was performing disproportionately well as a generator of new jobs. For countries concerned about the pace of job growth, this is a crucial message indeed.

Volunteers

In addition to their paid employees, nonprofit organizations benefit from the input of numerous volunteers, as noted above. These volunteers add significantly to nonprofit activity and output even though they do not show up on payrolls or expenditures.

To assess this "added dimension" of nonprofit operations, we commissioned specially targeted surveys in Germany, France, and Italy, and combined these with existing surveys of giving and volunteering in the United States.[2] We then blew the results of these surveys up to estimate the total contribution of volunteer effort to the labor available to the nonprofit sector in these countries.

Based on this analysis, we found that volunteers added the equivalent of an additional 4.7 million full-time employees to the nonprofit sector in these four countries alone. This represented an increase of over two-thirds beyond the amount of paid labor available. Quite clearly, volunteer effort significantly boosts the impact of the nonprofit sector well above what even the payrolls and expenditures of these organizations already indicate.

The nonprofit sector in the developing countries

Detailed employment and expenditure figures on the nonprofit sector are much more difficult to obtain in the developing

Table 2.4

Nonprofit organizations in developing countries

Country	Number of organizations
Brazil	190,086
Egypt	19,348
Thailand	10,854

Source: Johns Hopkins Comparative Nonprofit Sector Project

countries. Nevertheless, we were able to assemble important new data on these societies as well, and the picture that emerges also suggests a sector that is more extensive than commonly thought. In particular, as shown in Table 2.4:

- 45,000 nonprofit organizations have been identified in São Paolo, Brazil, and another 16,000 in Rio de Janeiro. In Brazil as a whole, the number of nongovernmental organizations is close to 200,000.
- In Egypt, a survey of nonprofit organizations found some 20,000 such organizations in existence as of the early 1990s.
- In Thailand, Bangkok alone boasts approximately 2,200 nonprofit organizations, and close to 11,000 have been identified countrywide.

Summary

Despite the widespread assumption that the nonprofit sector disappeared with the rise of the modern welfare state, nonprofit organizations remain a vital force in most of the nations covered in this project. In fact, the nonprofit sector is a massive industry whose employment and expenditures exceed those of some of the world's largest businesses by several orders of magnitude. What is more, this sector has recently functioned as a crucial engine of job growth, contributing far more new jobs than its share of total employment would suggest. Whatever its social, moral, or political importance, the nonprofit sector is also important in purely economic terms. As such, it deserves far more attention than it has so far been able to attract.

Notes

1 The 4.6 percent of GDP reported in Table 2.3 is a *weighted average* computed by dividing the total nonprofit expenditures in the target countries by total gross domestic product in the same countries. This differs from the unweighted average reported in Chapter 3, which is computed by calculating the ratio of nonprofit expenditures to gross domestic product for each country separately, adding these ratios together for the seven countries, and then dividing this sum by the number of countries.

It is important to note that the ratio of non-profit operating expenditures to gross domestic product reported here is different from the "value added" by the nonprofit sector as used in national income accounting. To calculate the latter, it would be necessary to deduct from non-profit expenditures the cost of all products and services nonprofit organizations consume in generating their revenues (e.g., supplies, equipment, utilities, facilities). Though different from the national income measure, the ratio reported here is still valuable as an understandable way to put the economic activity of the nonprofit sector into context.

2 In Germany, we commissioned a survey of a random sample of 2,062 West German households through the Zentrum für Umfragen, Methoden und Analysen & Gesellschaft für Marketing, Kommunikations-, und Sozialforschung mbH. Sozialwissenschaften-Bus III/1992. In France, we collaborated with the Laboratoire d'Economie Sociale, Université de Paris I, Sorbonne and the Fondation de France in a survey conducted by I.L.S. of a random sample of 1,986 people. In Italy, we relied on a survey of over 10,000 nonprofit organizations conducted by the I.R.S. research institute in Milan. Finally, data on the U.S. were developed from a survey conducted by the Gallup Organization for Independent Sector of 2,671 randomly selected American adults, as reported in Virginia Hodgkinson and Murray Weitzman, *Giving and Volunteering in the United States* (Washington, D.C.: Independent Sector, 1992).

Chapter 3

VARIATIONS ON A THEME

If the nonprofit sector is a far more significant presence on the landscape of contemporary society than is commonly assumed, its scale and character nevertheless vary considerably from place to place. According to existing explanations, as we have seen, such variations should be related to the degree of cultural and ethnic heterogeneity among societies, the scale of government social welfare spending, the level of overall economic development, the nature of the prevailing legal system, and the nature of national traditions regarding the role of the state and the shape of governmental institutions.

To the extent these explanations hold, we would expect the nonprofit sector to be more highly developed in Italy than in France (because of the lower level of government social welfare spending in the former). Both Japan and France could be expected to have fairly small nonprofit sectors, the former because of its high degree of homogeneity and the latter because of its quite high level of government social welfare activity. The U.S. and the U.K., by contrast, could be expected to have somewhat larger nonprofit sectors, both because of their common law legal traditions and, in the case of the United States, because of its relatively low level of government social welfare spending.

How well do these expectations stand up in the light of the data we have assembled? How much variation is there in the size of the nonprofit sector among countries? And to what extent do the factors introduced above seem to account for these variations?

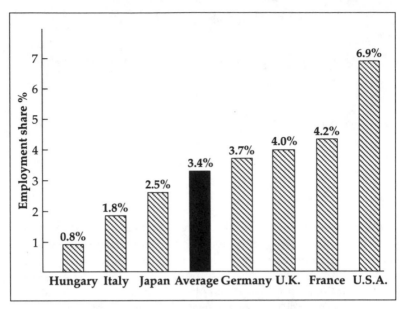

Figure 3.1   Nonprofit sector employment as % of total employment

Employment shares

As a first step toward answering these questions, we examined the share of the workforce that is employed in the nonprofit sector in each of the seven countries for which we were able to compile complete empirical data. The results, recorded in Figure 3.1, are intriguing and significantly at odds with what some of the prevailing theories would predict. For one thing, the degree of variation among countries is considerably smaller than conventional wisdom would suggest. Although the nonprofit share of total employment is clearly higher in the United States than in the other countries (6.9 percent as compared to the seven-country average of 3.4 percent), the major European countries covered, except for Italy, are not far behind, with employment in nonprofit organizations equal to about 4 percent of the total. In fact, nonprofit employment in France exceeds that in both Italy and the U.K. even though France has a more fully developed state welfare sector. What is more, even in Japan, a highly homogeneous country not generally regarded as a center of nonprofit

34

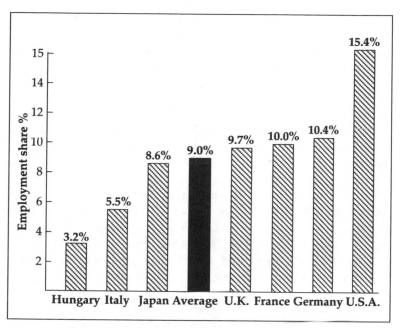

Figure 3.2 Nonprofit employment as a share of total service employment*, seven countries

* ISIC 8,9: Government, Business and Personal Services

activity, nonprofit organizations still account for 2.5 percent of total employment. Given the size of the Japanese economy, moreover, this translates into a substantial employment base, as we will see more fully below.

The significance of the nonprofit employment base in most of the countries covered in this project is even more clearly apparent when we relate nonprofit employment not to total employment, but to total service sector employment since this is the area where nonprofit organizations generally work. Thus, as Figure 3.2 shows, while the nonprofit share of service-sector employment ranges from a low of 3.2 percent in Hungary to a high of 15.4 percent in the United States, it falls in the relatively high range of 9–10 percent in most of the countries covered. Even in Japan, where the nonprofit share of total employment was below average, the nonprofit share of service sector employment is on a par with that in the U.K., France, and Germany. This is so because the service sector is a somewhat smaller part of the Japanese economy overall. For the seven countries taken as a whole, an average of 9 percent, or one in 11, of the increasingly important service jobs are in the nonprofit sector.

Three patterns

Although the nonprofit share of total employment, and of total service sector employment, is surprisingly significant in most of the countries covered, it is possible to group the countries into three broad categories in terms of the share of national employment accounted for by their nonprofit sectors. In the first category is the United States, with close to 7 percent of its total jobs, and one in seven of its service sector jobs, in the nonprofit sector. France, Germany, and the U.K. form a middle group with 3–4 percent of total employment, and 9–10 percent of service sector employment, in the nonprofit sector. Japan, Italy, and Hungary are at the low end, with 1–3 percent of their total employment in nonprofit organizations, although, as we have seen, in terms of the share of service sector employment only, Japan falls into the middle group.

Challenge to theories

While these groupings fit our theoretical expectations reasonably well, there are also anomalies. Thus France, Germany, and the U.K. turn out to have roughly comparably sized nonprofit sectors despite significant disparities in legal traditions, government structures, and levels of reliance on the state for social welfare protection. Indeed, instead of having a relatively smaller nonprofit sector than Germany or the U.K., as we would expect given its high level of government social welfare expenditure, France has a nonprofit sector that is slightly larger than the U.K.'s and on a par with Germany's. In addition, Japan, which we would expect to have a very limited nonprofit sector in view of its cultural homogeneity and heavy reliance on either government or private businesses for social welfare protection, turns out to have a nonprofit sector whose share of overall service sector employment is on a par with the Western European countries. Finally, even in Hungary, where the development of the nonprofit sector was stunted during the 40 years of Communist control, nonprofit organizations already account for over 3 percent of the service jobs.

What these findings seem to suggest is that a significant range of organized private activity outside both the market and the state may be a basic need in advanced, democratic societies regardless of other social or institutional features. Beyond this, as will become clear in Chapter 4, many of the anomalies that seem to exist may result from differences in the basic *composition* of the nonprofit sector in the different countries. In other words, the data on the sector as a whole may disguise important variations at the level of particular subsectors, such as health, education, and recreation. Even if this is the case, however, these data raise some questions about the standard theories that have been used to explain the presence or absence of nonprofit organizations among different countries. Most centrally, they pose a challenge to what might be termed the conflict theories, which see a conflict between the state and the nonprofit sector, and predict that the nonprofit sector will be large only where government spending is limited. In the process, these findings lend credence to an alternative theory that sees government and the nonprofit sector as potential partners and allies, a point to which we will return in Chapter 5.[1]

Expenditure shares

A similar pattern is evident in the data on nonprofit expenditures, though with some notable differences. As a share of gross domestic product, nonprofit expenditures vary from 1.2 percent in Hungary to 6.3 percent in the U.S. (See Figure 3.3.) What is most notable about these data, however, is not the extent of variation but the degree of similarity among the more developed countries and the sizable scale of the nonprofit sector that the data reveal. For all of the countries for which relevant data are available, the estimates we have developed reveal a nonprofit sector that is orders of magnitude larger than what OECD national income data suggest. Thus, where the OECD reported the French nonprofit sector as of 1990 to be a mere 0.26 percent of gross domestic product,[2] our data reveal a nonprofit sector in France with expenditures that are more than 15 times larger, or

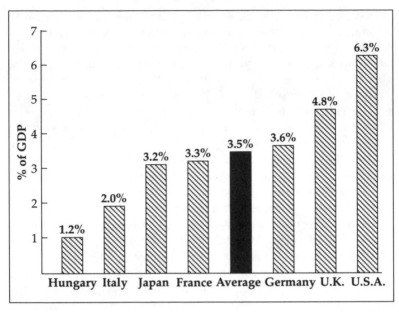

Figure 3.3   Nonprofit sector operating expenditures as percentage of gross domestic product

3.3 percent of gross domestic product. More generally, the nonprofit sector as it emerges from the data we have assembled represents 3–5 percent of gross domestic product in most of the countries covered, as compared to the 1–2 percent range suggested in earlier studies.[3] As will become clear below, however, this apparent similarity in overall scale disguises significant variations in the composition of this sector in the different countries.

Absolute size

Employment

Quite apart from the *relative* size of the nonprofit sector in the varying countries is the question of the *absolute* size. Because economies vary so greatly in size, 4 percent of one economy can translate into far more resources and jobs than 5 percent of another.

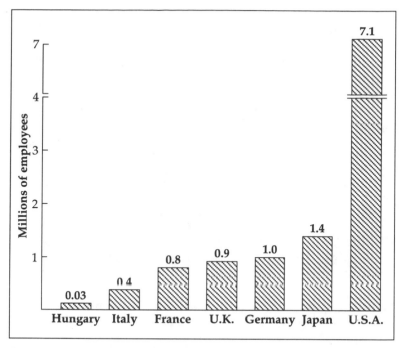

Figure 3.4 Nonprofit employment (millions)

As Figure 3.4 shows, in fact, the ranking of countries in terms of *absolute* size of their nonprofit sectors differs significantly from the ranking in terms of *relative* size. Most strikingly, while the U.S. remains in first place with over 7 million workers employed in its nonprofit sector, Japan turns out to be the second largest, with 1.4 million workers employed in nonprofit organizations. This means that there are 50 percent more jobs in the Japanese nonprofit sector than in the nonprofit sectors of Germany or the U.K., and almost twice as many as in the nonprofit sector of France. For those accustomed to think of Japan as a country with limited nonprofit activity, this is a striking finding indeed.

The absolute scale of the nonprofit sector is also quite impressive in relation to employment in the largest private companies in these countries. Thus, as Table 3.1 shows, not only does the American nonprofit sector employ 10 times more people than the world's largest private corporation (General Motors), but the

Table 3.1

Nonprofit employment in relation to employment in major corporations

Country	Largest private employer		Nonprofit employment	Ratio of nonprofit employment to employment of largest private firm
	Name	Number of employees		
France	Alcatel-Alsthom	213,000	802,619	3.8
Germany	Daimler-Benz	381,000	1,017,945	2.7
Italy	Fiat	128,000	416,383	3.2
Japan	Hitachi	274,000	1,440,228	5.2
U.K.	Unilever	298,000	945,883	3.2
U.S.	General Motors	717,000	7,130,826	9.9
Total		2,011,000	11,786,620	5.9

French nonprofit sector employs nearly 4 times more people than does the huge electronic conglomerate Alcatel-Alsthom, France's largest employer; the U.K. nonprofit sector employs over three times as many people as Unilever; the Japanese nonprofit sector employs five times more people than Hitachi; and the German nonprofit sector three times more than Daimler-Benz, maker of the Mercedes.[4] In short, the nonprofit economy outdistances the world's largest firms in terms of the jobs it provides, and this is true in virtually every one of the countries we examined.

Expenditures

A similar picture emerges from an analysis of the absolute expenditures of nonprofit organizations in the respective countries. As Figure 3.5 shows, in absolute terms, the United States has the largest nonprofit sector of the countries under consideration here, with expenditures of 272 billion ECU, or $346.4 billion. The second largest nonprofit economy, however, is that in Japan, which expended 74.7 billion ECU ($94.11 billion) in 1990.

Interestingly, nonprofit expenditures also exceed the gross sales of some of the large companies identified earlier. Thus the $346.4 billion in nonprofit expenditures in the United States exceeds the

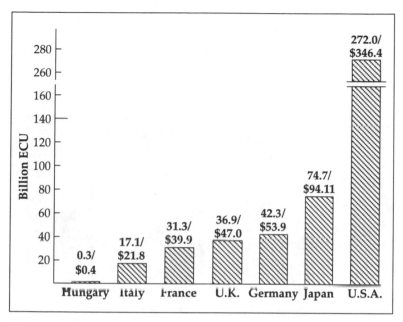

Figure 3.5   Nonprofit expenditure (1990), (billions ECU/U.S.$)

gross sales of General Motors by almost 3:1. Similarly in the U.K., nonprofit expenditures are 60 percent higher than the sales revenue of Unilever.

Job creation

Not only is the nonprofit sector an important employer, but its contribution to job creation has been increasing, as we noted in Chapter 2. In fact, the sector's contribution to job creation seems consistently high in all the countries on which we were able to compile time-series data. Thus, as shown in Figure 3.6, nonprofit organizations accounted for one out of every seven net new jobs created in the French economy during the 1980s, and one out of every eight to nine net new jobs created in the German and U.S. economies. Coupled with the evidence of overall employment size presented above, this is further powerful evidence of the economic importance of these organizations.

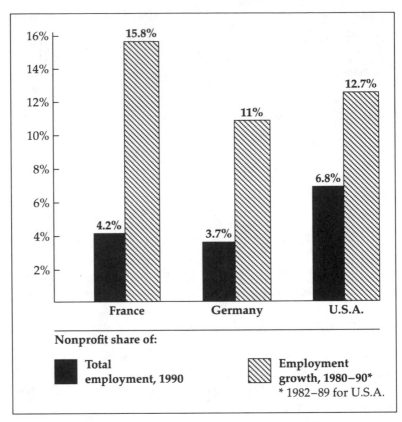

Figure 3.6   Nonprofit contribution to employment growth

Conclusion

Significant variations exist in the scale of nonprofit activity from country to country. Generally speaking, among the countries examined here, the nonprofit sector seems largest in the United States and smallest in Hungary, whether measured in absolute or relative terms or in terms of employment or expenditures. This pattern makes considerable sense given the severe limitations placed on the development of the nonprofit sector in Hungary during the era of Communist control and the relatively low level of state welfare provision in the United States. Somewhat more surprising is the limited scale of the nonprofit sector in

Italy. This likely reflects in part the heritage of conflict between the state and the Catholic Church in Italy during the late 19th century, which culminated in the state's takeover of the Church's network of social welfare institutions (the *Opere Pie*) in the *legge Crispi* of 1890.[5]

What is most surprising about the data reported in this chapter, however, is not the extent of variation in the scale of the nonprofit sector among the countries examined here, but the extent of similarity. At the aggregate level at least, the nonprofit sector turns out to be a very significant "industry" in most of the countries studied, accounting for at least twice the share of gross domestic product than has been commonly assumed, providing on average one in every 11 jobs in the increasingly important service sector, and generating more than one in every 10 net new jobs created over the decade of the 1980s. Though long neglected in government policy and public debate, the nonprofit sector has quietly taken its place as a significant economic, and not just social and moral, force in a wide assortment of different settings.

One possible explanation of this somewhat surprising finding may be that the aggregate picture of the nonprofit sector presented here disguises variations at the subsector level among the many different types of nonprofit organizations that exist in each country. To examine this possibility, we turn in the next chapter from the aggregate scale of this sector to the scale of its component parts, both generally and in our separate project countries.

Notes

1 For a statement of this partnership theory, see Lester M. Salamon, "Of Market Failure, Government Failure, and Third-Party Government: Toward a Theory of Government-Nonprofit Relations in the Modern Welfare State," *Journal of Voluntary-Action Research*, Vol. 16, Nos. 1–2 (January-June 1987), pp. 29–49. See also Lester M. Salamon, *Partners in Public Service: Government and the Nonprofit Sector in the Modern Welfare State* (Baltimore: Johns Hopkins University Press, 1995).

2 Organization of Economic Cooperation and Development (OECD), *National Accounts, Detailed Tables, 1976–1988* (Paris: OECD, 1991), Table 9.

3 It should be noted that our data relate GDP to *total nonprofit*

expenditures and not just to the *value-added* by the nonprofit sector as in the OECD data. Nevertheless, this does not come close to explaining the wide gap in the estimates.

4 Data on employment of private business firms from: Dun & Bradstreet, *Principal International Businesses: The 1994 Marketing Directory.* (Bethlehem, PA: Dun & Bradstreet Corporation, 1994).

5 Gian Paolo Barbetta, "Defining the Nonprofit Sector: Italy," in Lester M. Salamon and Helmut K. Anheier, eds., *Working Papers of the Johns Hopkins Comparative Nonprofit Sector Project*, No. 8 (Baltimore: The Johns Hopkins Institute for Policy Studies, 1993), pp. 2–3.

Chapter 4

A HOUSE WITH MANY ROOMS

Although the organizations that comprise the nonprofit sector share many common features, as noted in Chapter 1, they also have many differences. Indeed, tremendous diversity characterizes this sector, so much so that some observers question whether it is possible to talk about a coherent sector at all. Even when we limit our attention to the formal, nongovernmental, non-profit-distributing organizations other than churches and political organizations that have been our principal focus here, the range of organizational types and areas of activity is vast. In a sense, the nonprofit sector is a house with many rooms, and the configuration of these rooms can differ widely from country to country even though the external dimensions of the building appear very similar.

To cope with this reality, we developed a universal classification scheme to sort organizations in terms of their principal field of activity. As outlined in Chapter 1 above, and in Appendix B, this classification system, the International Classification of Nonprofit Organizations, or ICNPO, identifies 12 major "groups" of nonprofit organizations, 10 of which are covered here.[1]

In this chapter, we go beyond the measures of aggregate sector size presented in Chapters 2 and 3 to examine the scale of nonprofit activity in each of these fields, both overall and in the different countries. As before, we measure activity in terms of operating expenditures while recognizing that this may understate the true impact of the nonprofit sector, which draws as well on unpaid voluntary inputs.[2] Where possible, however, we indicate how the inclusion of volunteer effort would alter the overall

picture, drawing on surveys of volunteer activity that we conducted in several project countries. What emerges most clearly
from this analysis is the conclusion that the nonprofit "house,"
despite important differences, has a similar basic configuration
of major "rooms" from place to place. The "variations on a theme"
that was the principal message of Chapter 3's analysis of the
aggregate scale of the nonprofit sector in different countries turns
out to characterize the internal design of this sector in different
countries as well. To see this, we first look at the average composition of the nonprofit sector in our seven-country sample and
then examine how this varies from country to country.

The aggregate picture

As Figure 4.1 indicates, nonprofit expenditures are not distributed evenly among the 10 fields of activity identified in our classification system. To the contrary, four fields—education and
research, health, social services, and culture and recreation—turn
out to absorb the lion's share of nonprofit expenditures in the
seven countries we have examined in greatest depth. Altogether,
these four fields account for an average of over 80 percent of
total nonprofit spending in these seven countries. By contrast,
the other seven fields together contribute an average of less than
18 percent of the total.

Education and research

Of these four fields, education and research alone accounts for
nearly a quarter of total nonprofit spending on average. Most of
this is post-secondary education, though private elementary and
secondary schools are also quite common in some countries.

Health

Health is the second largest field of nonprofit activity in expenditure terms. On average, just over 20 percent of nonprofit spending goes for health services in these seven countries, most of it
through hospitals and clinics.

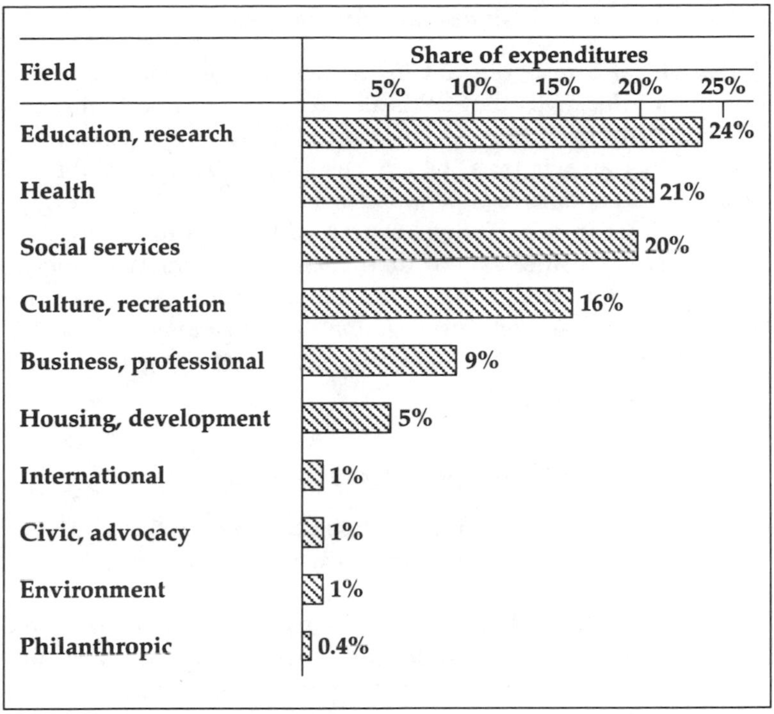

Field	Share of expenditures				
	5%	10%	15%	20%	25%
Education, research					24%
Health				21%	
Social services				20%	
Culture, recreation			16%		
Business, professional	9%				
Housing, development	5%				
International	1%				
Civic, advocacy	1%				
Environment	1%				
Philanthropic	0.4%				

Figure 4.1 Composition of the nonprofit sector, seven-country average

Social services

The third largest share of nonprofit spending goes for a wide assortment of social services. Included here are family counseling, crisis intervention, drug treatment, child day care, information and referral, and other similar services. Such services absorb on average 20 percent of nonprofit expenditures.

Culture and recreation

Finally, about 16 percent of nonprofit spending goes for culture and recreation. Included here are orchestras and art galleries, as well as sports clubs and the *tourisme social*, or social tourism clubs, common in France.

Business and professional

Although far less significant in financial terms than these four dominant fields, two other fields also account for important shares of nonprofit expenditures. The first of these are business and professional associations, which absorb an average of about 9 percent of all nonprofit expenditures. In some sense, these organizations differ from the others examined here because they principally serve the interests of their members rather than society more generally. Yet, in many developing countries and some developed ones as well, professional organizations such as bar associations also play a public role, defending the general right to free speech and assembly.

Development and housing

The other type of nonprofit agencies in this second tier are development and housing organizations, which account for an average of 5 percent of nonprofit expenditures in these seven developed countries. These organizations are principally involved in the provision of housing for the poor. Though considerably less prominent than organizations specializing in health, education, or social services in these seven developed countries, this category of organizations is far more important in the developing world, where it embraces a broad array of nongovernmental organizations, or NGOs. Reflecting the less specialized character of the nonprofit sector in the developing world, where the principal function of a health organization may be to develop a new water supply, the NGO category is a much broader catchall in these countries. As a result, it is a much larger component of the nonprofit sector in these countries than the seven country averages here might suggest. In Egypt, for example, a quarter of all nonprofit organizations we surveyed turned out to fall into this category.

Other

Aside from these fields, only three other types of nonprofit organizations absorb as much as 1 percent of average nonprofit expenditures: civic and advocacy organizations, international assistance organizations, and environmental organizations. The relatively small scale of the former suggests that while advocacy may be an important function of this sector, specialized advocacy organizations are not that common. With regard to the latter, while nonprofit organizations may be important in the international relief field, this field still constitutes a relatively small one compared to the domestic functions of the nonprofit sector in most of these countries.

Volunteer activity

The overall picture of the composition of nonprofit activity presented here does not change substantially when account is taken of the input of volunteers. Based on surveys of volunteer activity in four project countries—France, Germany, Italy, and the U.S.— the four major fields of nonprofit action identified above remain the principal fields even after taking account of volunteer inputs. At the same time, the inclusion of volunteer effort does have some impact on the results. In particular, the shares of total nonprofit resources devoted to culture and recreation, the environment, and civic and advocacy activity are noticeably higher with volunteer effort included than when we focus on operating expenditures alone.[3] This reflects the involvement of volunteers in sports, advocacy, and community organization activities. In the process, it demonstrates one of the strengths of the nonprofit sector as a vehicle for promoting individual self-expression and citizen activism, both of them crucial for a functioning civil society.

Variations by country

Interestingly, the aggregate picture of the structure of the nonprofit sector described above is strikingly consistent across the different countries. In all seven countries, therefore, the four dominant fields noted above—education and research, health, social services, and culture/recreation—account for at least three-fourths of all nonprofit expenditures.

At the same time, however, the relative importance of these four fields differs widely among the countries. In fact, a number of different patterns are apparent among these seven countries in terms of the dominant types of nonprofit organizations. What is more, even where two countries share the same dominant type of nonprofit organization, significant variations can exist in the specific subtypes of organizations that are responsible for this pattern. To see this, let us examine some of these patterns in more detail.

Japan and the U.K.: education-dominant

In two of our project countries, Japan and the U.K., education organizations dominate the nonprofit sector in terms of expenditures. As shown in Figure 4.2, and in more detail in Appendix D, 42 percent of all nonprofit expenditures in the U.K., and 40 percent of all nonprofit expenditures in Japan, go for education and research.

Important differences exist in the types of educational institutions that account for this pattern between these two countries, however. In the U.K., nonprofit organizations are prominently involved in both higher education and elementary and secondary education. The latter include the well-known fee supported "public schools," such as Eton and Harrow. So far as the former is concerned, most traditional British universities, such as Oxford, Cambridge and Manchester have long been part of what we are here terming the nonprofit sector, though much of their funding comes from the central government through a "quasi-nongovernmental organization" (or quango). As part of its privatization policies in the 1980s, however, the Thatcher government greatly expanded the nonprofit involvement in British higher education through the Education Acts of 1988 and 1992, which converted hundreds of colleges and polytechnics that had been run by local authorities into nonprofit organizations. As "new" universities, these institutions now enjoy the same legal status as the "old" universities and are funded through the same quango.

In Japan, the history of nonprofit involvement in education is even more complex. Private schools at the elementary, secondary, and collegiate level have long existed in Japan. Because of the importance of education to the modernization efforts launched by the Meiji government in the late 19th century, however, the authorities steadily tightened their controls over nonprofit private

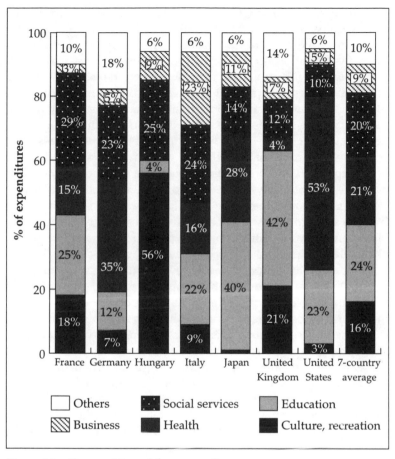

Figure 4.2 Composition of the nonprofit sector

education. Thus, while in the early part of this period private schools were just required to register themselves with the Ministry of Education, after 1911, when the Private Schools Order was amended, private schools were required to secure the approval of the minister before being established. They were also required to incorporate themselves as foundations, or *zaidan hō jin*, which strengthened their financial base but also subjected them to tighter governmental control. Governmental authorities were even empowered to dismiss teachers.[4]

In the postwar period, the position of private schools improved dramatically, though, as is generally true of the nonprofit sector in Japan, government supervision remains quite pronounced. Thus, the Private Schools Law of 1949 assigned these institutions equal status with government schools and required that they establish themselves as private school corporations, or *gakko hōjin*, to safeguard their autonomy and financial stability. In addition, private schools were offered the possibility of governmental support. At the same time, however, private schools must secure the approval of the Ministry of Education and Culture to be incorporated and are required to adhere to the guidelines laid down by this ministry with respect to curricula, facilities, teacher / student ratios, and the like. Overall, however, nonprofit organizations account for over 75 percent of all university education in Japan, and private institutions have proved increasingly popular at the elementary and secondary levels as well.

Beyond the common dominance of education organizations within the Japanese and U.K. nonprofit sectors, the nonprofit sectors in these countries differ quite markedly. Thus in the U.K., the second largest field of nonprofit activity in expenditure terms is culture and recreation. This reflects the presence of numerous social clubs, amateur sports clubs, and arts organizations such as museums and theaters. In addition, nonprofit organizations are disproportionately evident in the housing field in the U.K., reflecting the presence of a sizable number of nonprofit "housing associations" that manage a considerable, and growing, portion of the low-income rental housing market in the U.K. Finally, U.K. nonprofits are relatively more active than their counterparts in our other study countries in the fields of environment and international aid.

By contrast, the nonprofit sector is less significant a force in the U.K. than elsewhere in the fields of health and social services. The former reflects the creation in the immediate postwar period of the National Health Service, which transformed many nonprofit hospitals into state facilities. Were it not for this fact, the U.K. nonprofit sector would exceed the American in relative size. In addition, the U.K. boasts a substantial governmental system of personal social service provision, in this case run by local government. In both areas, however, recent changes are tending to increase reliance on nonprofit organizations. Thus, the 1990 health and community care legislation encouraged local government to contract with nonprofit and for-profit providers for a wide array of social care services.

In Japan, by contrast, the second largest area of nonprofit activity is health. As Figure 4.2 shows, 28 percent of all nonprofit expenditures in Japan go into health. Much of Japanese health care, in fact, is delivered by large, multipurpose, nonprofit "medical corporations," or *iryō hōjin*, usually under the close supervision of the Ministry of Health and Welfare. More than 7,000 such private medical corporations exist in Japan, operating hospitals, clinics, training institutes, and research centers.

Nonprofit organizations are much less heavily involved in the social services field in Japan, however, at least as compared to most of the European countries. A substantial number of private "social welfare corporations," or *shakaifukushi hōjin*, do exist in Japan, providing such services as care for the elderly, protection of women, maternal and child health, child day care, and assistance to the disabled. The estimated 12,000 such *shakaifukushi hōjin* nevertheless play a generally subsidiary role to that of the state. This follows from the stipulations of the Japanese Constitution, which assigns the state the primary role in social welfare protection. The *shakaifukushi hōjin* function, in fact, like quasi-governmental organizations performing certain tasks entrusted to them by central and local governments.[5] As concerns about the problems of the aged and other social issues grow in Japan, however, it seems likely that nonprofit involvement in this field will grow considerably, and with it a greater degree of nonprofit autonomy from the state.

U.S. and Germany: health-dominant

If education dominates the nonprofit sectors of Japan and the U.K., health dominates the nonprofit sectors of the United States and Germany. Over half (53 percent) of all nonprofit expenditures in the United States originate in the health field. This reflects the dominance of nonprofit organizations among American hospitals, over half of which are nonprofit in form. In Germany the health proportion of total nonprofit spending is somewhat smaller, but at 35 percent it still represents the largest single component. Much of this is in the hospital field, as in the United

States. Approximately one-third of all hospitals in Germany are operated by nonprofit organizations, most of them affiliated with the six large, religiously affiliated, nondenominational, or worker-based social welfare associations that make up much of the German nonprofit sector. In addition, however, about 6 percent of German nonprofit expenditures are in the field of nursing home care.

Except for their common emphasis on health care, however, the American and German nonprofit sectors diverge along other dimensions. Thus in the U.S., the second largest component of the nonprofit sector is education, mostly higher education. About half of all U.S. colleges and universities are nonprofit organizations, and these organizations account for 13 percent of all nonprofit expenditures. Another 10 percent of these expenditures are made by primary and secondary schools and research institutes. Altogether, therefore, over three-fourths of all nonprofit expenditures in the U.S. flow into these two fields. By comparison, the share of nonprofit expenditures in the other fields in the U.S. lags behind the seven-country average. Particularly noteworthy is the relatively small share that goes for culture and recreation and for social services. With regard to the former, the principal reason appears to be the fact that sports and recreation clubs that in other countries are part of the nonprofit sector are more commonly for-profit businesses in the U.S. Although most U.S. orchestras, art galleries, and museums are nonprofit, the overall culture and recreation share of nonprofit expenditures in the U.S. is smaller than it is elsewhere. So far as the social service share is concerned, this reflects as much the huge scale of the hospital sector as a share of the total as it does the limited scale of nonprofit involvement in social services in the U.S. In fact, when measured as a percent of gross domestic product, as opposed to as a percent of total nonprofit expenditures, nonprofit social service activity in the U.S. is slightly above the seven-country average.

For Germany, the second most important area of nonprofit activity is not education, as in the U.S., but social services. In substantial part, this reflects the powerful German policy of "subsidiarity," which obliges government to place primary reliance on nonprofit organizations to deliver human services. This policy has helped to sustain a network of six large social welfare associations in Germany, each of which operates a substantial network of human service agencies.[6] Reflecting this, almost a quarter of all nonprofit expenditures in Germany are made by social service organizations. Beyond this, Germany also boasts a disproportionately large nonprofit sector in the field of housing and development. Over 15 percent of total sector spending falls into this field. Rooted in the labor movement's efforts to improve the housing of the working class in Germany in the 1920s, nonprofit involvement grew rapidly in response to the housing crisis that existed after World War II. Indeed, an entire public-interest housing construction sector, or *Gemeinnütziger Wohnungsbau*, was created to build and rent housing for low-income people. More recently, however, a number of scandals among these nonprofit housing companies have prompted the conservative Kohl government to move against these institutions. In 1989, therefore, the government passed legislation that changed these associations to for-profit corporations. The figures shown here, therefore, are very much in a state of flux and the housing component of the nonprofit sector in Germany has now declined quite markedly. Thus, while 17.5 percent of all German housing units were owned by such nonprofit housing corporations as of 1989, the rate had fallen to under 2 percent by 1990.[7]

France and Italy: social service-dominant

A third pattern of nonprofit sector structure is evident in France and Italy, where the social service field dominates nonprofit expenditures. Thus almost 30 percent of French nonprofit expenditures and about a quarter of Italian nonprofit expenditures are made by social service agencies, as Figure 4.2 shows. In France, this reflects the presence of such emergency relief networks as *Secours Catholique* and the socialist-inspired *Secours Populaire*, as well as the numerous agencies that are part of UNIOPSS, the French union of human service organizations. These organizations have benefited greatly from a significant shift in government policy in the early 1980s, which reversed a long-standing pattern of centralized control of social policy in France and gave new powers to local government. As part of this shift, the Decentralization Law of 1982 explicitly authorized local authorities to enlist private nonprofit organizations in the provision of social welfare services. This has since been further reinforced by laws relating to worker training and "minimum insertion income," the latter of which opens a significant role for nonprofit organizations in implementing "insertion contracts" designed to put disadvantaged people on the road to self-support.[8]

A similar set of changes has also been under way in Italy, though there the story is complicated by a recent shift in what has long been the curious legal status of many nonprofit social welfare agencies. Under the *legge Crispi* enacted in 1890, as we have seen, Italy's church-affiliated *Opere Pie* organizations were essentially nationalized and converted into *Istituzioni Pubbliche di Assistenza e Beneficenza* (public charity and assistance institutions), or IPABs. But things are never quite what they seem in Italy, and the IPABs continued to be operated by the Church even though they were formally instruments of the state. Their role grew, however, as a result of a decentralization effort begun in 1977 that made local governments responsible for health and social services. Lacking institutional structures through which to deliver such services, local governments have turned extensively to the IPABs and other private institutions. More recently, the ambiguous legal position of the IPABs has been partially clarified thanks to a 1988 ruling of the Italian Constitutional Court that invalidated the *legge Crispi* and opened the way for IPABs to reestablish themselves formally as private institutions.[9]

Other features of the French and Italian nonprofit sectors are also strikingly similar, moreover. Thus, for both, the nonprofit sector is also fairly substantial in the field of education. Unlike in the U.K. and Japan, however, it is not higher education that absorbs nonprofit energies in the educational field. Rather, in the case of France, it is elementary and secondary education, much of it through church-related schools. In the case of Italy it is church-related elementary and secondary education as well as the new field of vocational education. This latter is an outgrowth of Italy's Law 845 of 1978, which established a system of private vocational training and educational centers for Italy's small and medium-sized industries. Though financed by public funds, much of it from the European Community, these centers are structured as nonprofit organizations to avoid competition with businesses. In fact, Italy's strong unions and professional associations took a very active role in creating many of the nonprofit training institutes that resulted from this new law. The Italian vocational education centers thus demonstrate the important role that the nonprofit sector can play where the public sector finds it necessary to add an important function but lacks the institutional infrastructure with which to do so.

While sharing a sizable nonprofit presence in the fields of social services and education, France and Italy also share relatively limited nonprofit involvement in the field of health. Although 15–17 percent of nonprofit expenditures fall into the health field in these two countries, this is far lower than in most of the other countries except for the U.K. This is so because much of the expansion of hospital care in these countries has occurred through public institutions, with private, often church-related institutions playing a much smaller role.[10]

The composition of the French and Italian nonprofit sectors does diverge in two significant respects, however. In the first place, a much larger share of French nonprofit expenditures originates in the field of culture and recreation. For the most part, this reflects the important role of sports clubs and culture and multipurpose facilities initiated in the 1950s by André Malraux, the first minister of culture. Also important are the *tourisme social*, or social tourism clubs, which were formed at the instigation of Socialist Minister Leo Lagrange beginning in the 1930s, when the first "vacation with pay" was established to make it possible for French workers to enjoy their new free time. Following World War II, this network of youth hostels and holiday villages expanded considerably, with government assistance, to provide tourism and recreational opportunities for working and middle-income people. The resulting social tourism clubs constitute a distinctive part of the French nonprofit sector today.[11] A similar phenomenon is evident in the *clubs du troisième âge*, or clubs for the elderly. These uniquely French institutions make use of the nonprofit sector to provide enrichment experiences for French citizens.

If the culture and recreation component of the nonprofit sector is larger in France than in Italy, the business and professional component is larger in Italy than in France. Several factors seem to account for this. In the first place, Italy has an unusually high rate of union membership (70 percent of total employees). This reflects in part the influence of Law 300 of 1970, which required the state to support unions. Also important is the "corporatist" structure of Italian society, the pattern of close working relations between professional associations and political parties. Coupled with the relatively small size of Italian firms, which places a special premium on the formation of networks and associations, the result is a highly structured world of business, union, and professional organizations. Similar forces are evident in other countries as well, of course, particularly Germany, but in the context of the smaller overall size of the nonprofit sector in Italy, they take on special importance.

Hungary: culture-dominant

Finally, a wholly different pattern of nonprofit sector structure is evident in Hungary. There, as Figure 4.2 indicates, the overwhelming majority (56 percent) of all nonprofit expenditures are in the culture and recreation component of the sector. This reflects the presence of sports clubs, recreation and hobby clubs even during the Communist era, as well as efforts of cultural ministries in the waning years of Communist rule to retain control of the cultural sector by establishing a number of large foundations to support cultural activities. Because of the limited funds available to support nonprofit activity in Hungary in other fields, these cultural institutions bulk large in the expenditure structure of the Hungarian nonprofit sector. More recently, as part of its effort to privatize the economy, the post-Communist government in Hungary has enacted legislation authorizing local authorities to contract with nonprofit organizations in the human service field. As a consequence, this is the one other field where substantial nonprofit expenditures are also in evidence in Hungary. For the rest, however, the nonprofit sector in Hungary remains a much more voluntary enterprise, with far more limited financial resources.

Conclusion

If the nonprofit sector appears to be roughly comparable in aggregate scale among the countries examined here, its composition nevertheless differs considerably from country to country. This is, in fact, one of the great strengths of this set of institutions: its ability to adapt to local circumstances and respond to local needs. If the nonprofit sector provides a home for many crucial social functions, it is a house with many rooms, each of which reflects the architectural styles of particular national cultures.

The presence or absence of nonprofit activity is not, however, simply a by-product of gaps left by the state. This "gap-filling" conception of the nonprofit sector turns out not to fit the available evidence in any of the countries we have examined. While there are cases where the presence of the state has discouraged or displaced nonprofit action, there are at least as many cases where the opposite has occurred, where state involvement has stimulated nonprofit activity, and nonprofit organizations have facilitated the expansion of state-financed protections. To understand this point more fully, however, it is necessary to turn from this analysis of the expenditure side of nonprofit operations to an assessment of the revenue side instead.

Notes

1 In addition to the 12 "groups," the International Classification of Nonprofit Organizations (ICNPO) identifies 26 subgroups. The two groups not covered here are Group 10: Religion and Group 12: Other. In addition, subgroup 7–300 under Group 7: Law, Advocacy, and Politics is excluded, as noted in Chapter 1. For a full explanation of the considerations that went into the design of this classification system, see Lester M. Salamon and Helmut K. Anheier, "In Search of the Nonprofit Sector II: The Problem of Classification," *Voluntas*, Vol. 3, No. 3 (1992), pp. 267–309.

2 As a check on the expenditure figures, we also examined the distribution of nonprofit employment among the various fields and subfields. Since the results were quite close to those for expenditures, there was no point in presenting them separately. We do, however, report them in Appendix E. Another measure of the scope of nonprofit activity in a field is the number of organizations. Although we collected data on the number of organizations in each field, these data seem less reliable than the employment and expenditure data. We therefore decided against reporting them here. As a general rule, however, nonprofit health organizations are less numerous than their share of expenditures would suggest, while nonprofit social service and cultural and recreational organizations are more numerous.

3 The value of volunteer effort was calculated by assigning an imputed value to the hours that volunteers reported devoting to each of the fields of service. The imputed value was calculated using the

average wage in the country. With these imputed values included, the share of total nonprofit resources devoted to recreation in the four countries for which we have volunteer data climbs from 11 percent to 20 percent, the civic and advocacy share increases from 1 percent to 3 percent, and the environment share from 1 percent to 2 percent.

4 Takayoshi Amenomori, "Defining the Nonprofit Sector: Japan," in Lester M. Salamon and Helmut K. Anheier, eds., *Working Papers of the Johns Hopkins Comparative Nonprofit Sector Project*, No. 15 (Baltimore: The Johns Hopkins Institute for Policy Studies, 1993), pp. 10–11.

5 Amenomori, "Defining the Nonprofit Sector," p. 9.

6 These associations are Caritas (Catholic), Diakonisches Werk (Protestant), Arbeiterwohlfahrt (Workers' Welfare), Deutscher Paritätischer Wohlfahrtsverband, Deutsches Rotes Kreuz (Red Cross), and the Jewish Welfare Agency. In addition to their grant and contract receipts, the religiously affiliated networks receive support from the semi-voluntary "church tax," which is collected by the state and distributed to the major religious denominations to support both their religious functions and their educational and social-welfare functions.

7 Based on the data reported in Statistisches Bundesamt, *Bautätigkeit und Wohnungen*, Fachserie 5, Reihe 1, Tabelle 4.2 (Stuttgart: Metzler-Poeschel, 1991 and 1992).

8 Edith Archambault, "Defining the Nonprofit Sector: France," in Lester M. Salamon and Helmut K. Anheier, eds., *Working Papers of the Johns Hopkins Comparative Nonprofit Sector Project*, No. 7 (Baltimore: The Johns Hopkins Institute for Policy Studies, 1993), pp. 3, 21–22.

9 Gian Paolo Barbetta, "Defining the Nonprofit Sector: Italy," in Lester M. Salamon and Helmut K. Anheier, eds., *Working Papers of the Johns Hopkins Comparative Nonprofit Sector Project*, No. 8 (Baltimore: The Johns Hopkins Institute for Policy Studies, 1993), pp. 2, 3, 5.

10 The relative scale of the health subsector within the Italian nonprofit sector would increase slightly were we to shift some of the residential care facilities now grouped in social services into health as stipulated in our classification system. Because of the absence of suitable information to differentiate those residential care facilities that require skilled nursing care in Italy from those that do not, it is difficult to make this split precisely. Assuming a split roughly comparable to what exists in other countries, however, the health share of total nonprofit expenditure in Italy would increase from 16.4 percent to 21.5 percent, and the social services share would decline to 19.4 percent.

11 Archambault, "Defining the Nonprofit Sector: France," p. 21.

Chapter 5

NONPROFIT FINANCE

If the scale of the nonprofit sector differs from place to place in part because of variations in the sector's basic composition, it differs also because of variations in its sources of support. To be sure, nonprofit organizations are less vulnerable to the financial "bottom line" than many other types of institutions. They do not have profit-conscious private investors like for-profit companies and can tap significant reservoirs of voluntary effort to assist with organizational tasks.

Yet even nonprofit organizations must ultimately come to terms with the hard realities of finance. There are limits, after all, to what can be asked of volunteers. As nonprofit organizations grow in size and responsibilities, they therefore increase as well their need for financial support—to pay staff, secure space, acquire supplies, and generally run their operations. Under the circumstances, it is important to inquire how nonprofit organizations finance their activities. This is important not alone for descriptive purposes, but also for what it can suggest about the role these organizations play in different societies and the relationships that exist between them and other key sectors.

To examine these issues, we collected information on three broad classes of nonprofit revenue:

- First, *private charitable giving*, including gifts from individuals, corporations, foundations, and bequests, whether given directly or through various federated fundraising efforts;
- Second, *government support, or public sector payments*, including outright grants, as well as contracts for particular services and payments by public sector organizations to nonprofit providers

delivered to an eligible recipient or reimbursing the recipient;[1] and

- Third, *private fees and payments* that the nonprofit organization receives from the sale of its own services or of some other product directly to a consumer.[2]

The relative roles of these different funding sources can have significant implications for the structure and character of the nonprofit sector. It is important to know, therefore, what variations exist in the patterns of finance from country to country and from field to field.

To answer these questions, the discussion here falls into three basic parts. First, we examine the overall pattern of nonprofit finance for the countries on which we have collected empirical data. Next we assess the extent to which variations are apparent among the different countries and the implications that these variations might have. Finally, we examine the variations among service fields to determine whether there are distinctive patterns of nonprofit finance in different areas. Against this backdrop, we then examine the implications that seem to flow from these data for our overall understanding of this sector and the role it plays on the global level.

The aggregate picture

According to conventional wisdom, what sets the nonprofit sector apart from the government and business sectors is its reliance on private charitable giving, as opposed to public sector support or private fees, as its principal source of income. Indeed, as we have seen, this basic premise was built into the U.N. System of National Accounts, which defines a nonprofit organization as an organization that receives half or more of its income from private philanthropic sources as opposed to government or market sales.[3] Underlying this definition is an assumption of sharp divisions between the different sectors and little active cooperation among them.

In point of fact, however, this widespread assumption not only fails to come to terms with some of the dominant realities of nonprofit operations, but it does not even come close to the mark. To the contrary, as reflected in Figure 5.1, private giving is not

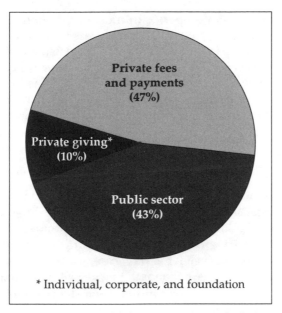

Figure 5.1 Sources of nonprofit revenue, seven-country average
Source: Johns Hopkins Comparative Nonprofit Sector Project

only not the major source of nonprofit income in our seven countries. It is not even the second most important. Rather, the average share of total nonprofit income originating with private philanthropic giving in the seven countries for which we collected comparable data was only 10 percent, most of it (about 60 percent) from individuals, with corporations and foundations providing most of the rest. By contrast, almost half (47 percent) of all nonprofit income in these seven countries comes on average from private fees and sales, and 43 percent from public sector payments.

How can we explain this pattern? And what does it suggest about the nature of this sector? Several observations seem in order here.

The market context

In the first place, the heavy reliance of nonprofit organizations on private fees and sales reflects the market context within which nonprofit organizations operate in most of the countries considered here. While nonprofit organizations are insulated from these market forces in part, they are hardly insulated totally. Where services are provided to clients who can pay, collecting fees becomes a matter of organizational necessity. Whether this distorts the service offerings or client focus of the nonprofit sector is difficult to determine, but the pressures in that direction must be real.

Changing demand for nonprofit services

Working to increase nonprofit reliance on private fees has been a set of social and economic trends that have broadened the demand for the kinds of services that nonprofits provide. Included here are the growing labor force participation of women, which increases the need for day care services; increased life expectancy, which has expanded the need for nursing homes and various forms of "community care" for the elderly; new medical technology, which has stimulated new demands for medical care; and changing skill requirements in the job market, which has put increased pressure on educational institutions.[4] While some of these pressures have been channeled to governmental and for-profit institutions, they also translate into demands for nonprofit services as well, and demands from "customers" who can often pay for the services they receive.

Growing doubts about the capacity of the state

Finally, the pattern of nonprofit finance reflected in Figure 5.1 also results from changing perceptions about the capacities of the modern welfare state and resulting changes in conceptions about the relationship between the state and the nonprofit sector. Where earlier sentiment looked to the state as the optimum provider of a wide range of social welfare benefits, recent years have given rise to fears that the welfare state may have taken on more than it can handle efficiently.[5] While some have responded to these fears by emphasizing the need to reduce the overall level of state-financed human services, others have argued instead for a sharing of responsibilities between the state and the nonprofit sector under which the state would continue to finance a growing array of social services but turn to nonprofit organizations for the actual delivery of the services. Far from the alternative to the welfare state emphasized in the heterogeneity and "government failure" theories outlined in Chapter 1, this view thus sees the nonprofit sector as a mechanism to facilitate the further expansion of welfare-state services. The result is an elaborate network of partnership arrangements between the nonprofit sector and the state. Such a pattern has long characterized government-nonprofit relations in Germany and the United States.[6] From the evidence here, it appears that it is increasingly important in other countries as well.

Variations among countries

While the pattern of nonprofit finance reported in Figure 5.1 seems quite clear, it is still possible that the aggregate averages reported here obscure important variations from place to place. To check on this, it is necessary to examine how the funding structure of the nonprofit sector varies by country.

Figure 5.2 reports the results of such an analysis (for a complete summary of the data on which this figure is based, see Appendix F). What it reveals are two broad patterns of nonprofit finance, one of which mirrors the overall pattern described above, and the other of which is a variation on it. In addition, this figure sheds light on the relatively limited role that private giving plays in financing nonprofit action.

Private fee-dominant pattern

Perhaps the central conclusion that flows from Figure 5.2 is the prevalence of the overall pattern of nonprofit finance reported above. Thus, of the seven countries examined here, five (Hungary, Italy, Japan, the U.K., and the U.S.) display a pattern of nonprofit finance that is in accord with the overall average. For all of these countries, the major source of nonprofit finance is private fees and payments, followed by public sector support and then private giving. Thus, earned income accounts for 60 percent of total nonprofit income in Japan, 57 percent in Hungary, 53 percent in Italy, and 52 percent in the United States. The

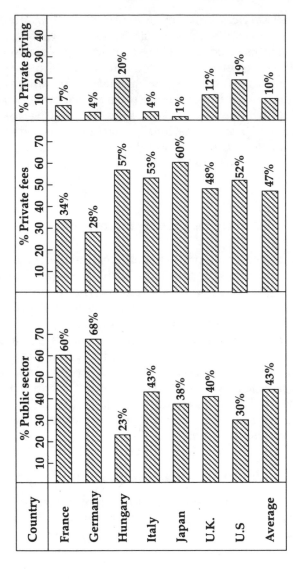

Figure 5.2 Sources of nonprofit revenue, by country

Source: Johns Hopkins Comparative Nonprofit Sector Project

U.S. figure is perhaps the most surprising in view of the assumptions about the role that private giving is supposed to play in the United States. As Figure 5.2 shows, however, while private giving represents a larger proportion of nonprofit income in the United States than it does in any other country but one, that proportion is still only 19 percent. By contrast, U.S. nonprofit organizations receive 52 percent of their income from private fees and another 30 percent from government. Government is thus almost twice as significant a source of income for American nonprofit organizations as is private giving, despite the presence there of numerous large foundations and corporate giving programs.[7]

Public sector dominant pattern

For the two remaining countries we have examined (Germany and France), private fees represent a smaller share of total nonprofit income. However, their role as the principal source of nonprofit finance is taken not by private philanthropy, but by government. Thus the public sector accounts for 68 percent of the income of German nonprofit organizations and 60 percent of the income of French nonprofit organizations. By contrast, private fees represent 28 percent and 34 percent of revenue, respectively, and private giving only 4 percent and 7 percent.

The overwhelming dominance of government in the funding of nonprofit organizations in Germany reflects the hold of the doctrine of "subsidiarity" in the German welfare state. The outgrowth of Catholic social doctrine in the 1930s, this principle was firmly enshrined in German social legislation in the aftermath of World War II. It essentially holds that before the state can enter a sphere of social or economic life, it must be sure that no smaller social unit—the family, the local community, or the voluntary group—can handle the function instead. What is more, when the state does enter a field, it must make every effort to involve these lower units. The result is an elaborate collaborative relationship between the state and a wide variety of nonprofit organizations in Germany to deal with youth problems, unemployment, care for the elderly, health care, and many other human services.[8]

Cooperation between the state and the nonprofit sector has historically been more limited in France, reflecting a long tradition of state hostility to voluntary associations fastened onto French society during the French Revolution. While early examples of such cooperation exist, such as the government-sponsored "social tourism" organizations established in the mid-1930s, it was not until the passage of the Decentralization Law of 1982 that a full-blown partnership was forged between the state and the voluntary sector. Confronted by strong resistance to the further extension of the welfare state, the Socialist government of François Mitterand essentially turned to the voluntary sector to facilitate the expansion of state-financed welfare services. As we have seen, the 1982 law therefore not only transferred significant social welfare responsibilities to local governments but also instructed these governments to enlist nonprofit organizations as partners in the exercise of these responsibilities.[9] Nonprofit organizations have consequently been deeply involved in French employment initiatives (*contrats emploi solidarité*) and a network of nonprofit *Entreprises Intermédiaires* (intermediary enterprises) have emerged to provide temporary jobs to unemployed youth and school dropouts. Similarly, as we have seen, nonprofit organizations have an important role in the new minimum income program for the poor enacted in 1989. Thanks to these and other efforts, the public sector has emerged as the principal source of nonprofit finance in France, outdistancing both private fees and private charity by a substantial margin. In most of the other countries as well, though government is not the principal source of nonprofit income, it is not far behind. Thus government accounts for between 38 and 43 percent of nonprofit revenue in Italy, the U.K., and Japan, and for around 30 percent in the U.S.

Private charity

Significantly, despite the widespread conventional impression, in none of the countries considered here is private charity the dominant source of nonprofit finance. Indeed, the highest that private giving reaches as a share of overall nonprofit income is 20 percent, and this is, ironically enough, in Hungary, the country where private giving operates from possibly the smallest base. However, much of this comes from enterprises that are still part of the public sector. Outside of Hungary, the highest that private giving reaches as a share of nonprofit income is in the U.S., where it is 19 percent. Elsewhere, private giving is even more limited—12 percent in the U.K., 7 percent in France, 4 percent in Germany, and about 1 percent in Japan.

One reason for the relatively limited availability of private giving in most of the countries examined here is the relatively high level of taxation that exists. Thus, compared to the 29 percent of national income that goes for taxes in the United States, the comparable rate in France is 42 percent, in Germany 40 percent, and in the U.K. 35 percent.[10] This is particularly problematic since the incentives for charitable contributions and for the formation of charitable foundations are generally far less supportive in these countries than they are in the United States. Thus, in the United States, individual charitable contributions are deductible from income before computing tax obligations through a relatively simple self-certification method and with rather generous limits.[11] In the U.K., however, a more cumbersome "covenanting" system is in place, requiring three-year commitments to make charitable contributions. What is more, the tax benefits flowing from contributions accrue to the charity rather than the contributor. Elsewhere, the incentives for charitable contributions are even less supportive.[12] Under these circumstances, it is understandable why citizens in these countries might conclude that they have already made their "contributions" through the state, leaving far less for nonprofit organizations to tap.

Reflecting this, a survey we conducted of giving and volunteering in Germany and France in 1991–1992 revealed that private individual giving represented rather minuscule levels of personal income. Thus, as shown in Figure 5.3, individual giving to other-than-religious nonprofit organizations amounted to only 0.15 percent of personal income for the sampled households in France and 0.31 percent for the sampled households in Germany.[13] The comparable U.S. figure, based on a virtually identical survey, was 1.9 percent—still below 2 percent of personal income, but proportionately three times higher than the German figure.[14] Although, like all population surveys, these surveys understate the contributions of high-income contributors, who tend to be underrepresented in survey work, the overall conclusion seems correct: though important for the independence of the nonprofit sector, individual giving everywhere is a limited basis for

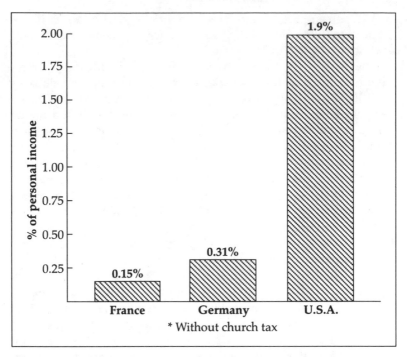

Figure 5.3   Individual giving as a share of personal income
Source: Johns Hopkins Comparative Nonprofit Sector Project

nonprofit action, and this is even more true in the highly developed welfare states of Europe and Asia than in the United States.

If individual giving is limited, however, other forms of private philanthropic support are even more limited. Thus, as shown in Table 5.1, only for the U.S. and the U.K., of the countries for which we were able to compile comparable data, do foundations provide as much as 2 percent of total nonprofit income. Corporate giving is somewhat more substantial, exceeding 2 percent of total income for three of the five countries. Particularly noteworthy here is the role that corporate giving plays in Hungary, though corporations here are still mostly state-owned enterprises.

The fact that foundations and corporations account for a relatively small share of total nonprofit income is not to say that they

Table 5.1

Private giving as a share of nonprofit income, by source and country

Source	% of total nonprofit income				
	France	**Germany**	**Hungary**	**U.K.**	**U.S.**
Individuals	3.8%	2.1%	5.3%	6.5%	13.9%
Foundations	0.4	0.6	0.8	2.4	2.0%
Corporations	2.9	0.7	9.6	2.8	1.8%
Other	—	0.5	4.0	0.3	0.9%
Total private giving	7.1%	3.9%	19.7%	12.0%	18.5%

Source: Johns Hopkins Comparative Nonprofit Sector Project

do not play immensely significant roles, particularly in certain fields. German foundations, for example, have been extremely important in the field of research. U.S. and U.K. foundations have been instrumental in stimulating new approaches to numerous social problems and in helping to finance advocacy for unpopular causes. And the *Fondation de France* has been instrumental in promoting the arts and encouraging social experimentation in a wide variety of areas. While the scale of private giving may lag behind what many would expect, therefore, the contributions that it makes can still be significant. At the same time, private giving is not sufficient to permit the nonprofit sector to take its place as a major "player" in the modern welfare state. For this, government involvement has been necessary.

Variations by field of nonprofit action

Since considerable variations exist in the composition of the nonprofit sector from country to country, it is at least possible that the country patterns examined above may still be a product not of differences among countries, but of differences in the funding structure of different types of nonprofit organizations. To assess this, we need first to see if variations exist in the funding structures for different types of agencies, and then examine what impact, if any, the country has on the outcome.

Funding structure by field

Figure 5.4 below records the funding structure for each of the 10 major types of nonprofit organizations covered in our project. What is apparent from this figure is that there are important differences among the different types of agencies. At the same time, however, the overall pattern discussed earlier holds for most of the major fields. In particular:

- In six of the 10 fields, *private fees* are the dominant source of income. This is true for business and professional associations (92 percent), culture and recreation (67 percent), philanthropic intermediaries (54 percent), environment (51 percent), education and research (50 percent), and housing and development (51 percent). For the most part these are easily understandable. Thus, for example, nonprofit business and professional associations receive dues from their members, cultural and recreational organizations charge fees for their services, and colleges and universities collect tuition payments from students. In the case of philanthropic intermediaries, the explanation is more complicated, reflecting the earnings these organizations receive on invested assets.
- For three of the fields, the public sector is the principal source of income. This is true in the fields of health (59 percent), social services (51 percent), and advocacy (49 percent). Beyond this, government is a major secondary player in at least three other fields (education, housing, and international development). This pattern reflects the significant public sector presence in social welfare and the growing practice of government reliance on nonprofit organizations to deliver social welfare services. The government support for nonprofit advocacy is more surprising and suggests a striking reality of the modern welfare state—that government agencies end up supporting nonprofit organizations that help advocate for their programs.
- Although in no field was *private giving* the dominant source of support, it came very close in the field of international assistance and here, it is slightly below the level of public sector assistance. Private giving also plays a major role, obviously, in supporting philanthropic intermediaries such as foundations, but these organizations receive significantly more of their income from earnings on past gifts than they do from current gifts.

72

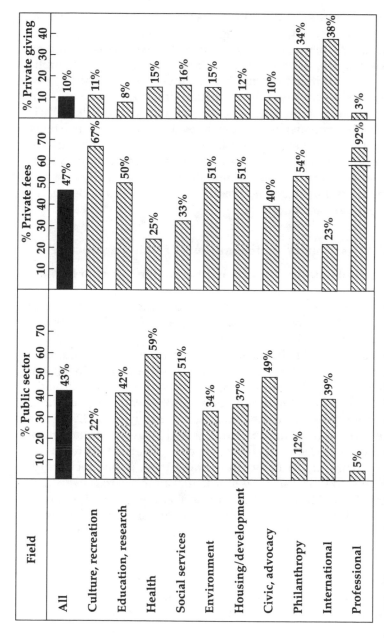

Figure 5.4 Sources of nonprofit revenue, by field (seven-country average)

Source: Johns Hopkins Comparative Nonprofit Sector Project

In short, significant variations do appear in the funding structures of different types of organizations. Generally speaking, organizations primarily engaged in social welfare and human service activities derive most of their income from the public sector. Organizations serving broad cross-sections of the population, such as cultural and recreation organizations, education organizations, and business associations, receive the bulk of their income from private fees and charges. Only international relief agencies receive most of their income from private giving, but they rely almost equally on government support. Though a relatively small share of total income, however, private giving can still be quite important in preserving a meaningful degree of nonprofit independence.

Field vs. country as determinants of funding structure

Since both the field of service and the country seem to have an influence on the funding structure of the nonprofit sector, it is important to sort out which of these is most important. To do this, Figure 5.5 zeroes in on just one type of nonprofit income—government support—and examines how it varies across the four largest service fields in the seven countries we have examined.

As this figure shows there are clearly variations in the extent of reliance on public sector support among these three fields. Thus, 59 percent of the income of nonprofit health organizations on average comes from the public sector compared to 22 percent of the income of nonprofit cultural and recreational organizations. At the same time, there are also distinctive patterns by country. Thus in Germany, France, and Italy, public sector support to the nonprofit sector is substantial almost across the board, By contrast, in Hungary, it is quite low almost across the board. The U.S., the U.K., and Japan are mixed cases, with areas of substantial government support (e.g., social services) and others (e.g., education and culture) where government support is well below average.

What these data suggest is that despite significant differences among service fields, there are also distinctive national "styles" in the financing of nonprofit activity. Particularly noticeable in this respect is the heavy reliance on the public sector as the financier of nonprofit activity in Germany, Italy, France, and, except

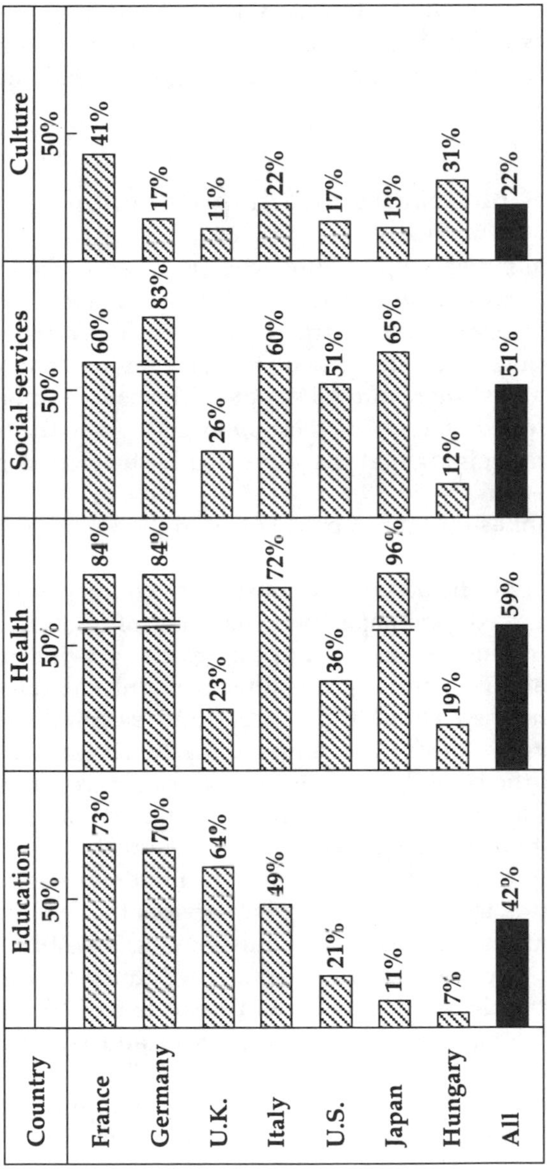

Country	Education 50%		Health 50%		Social services 50%		Culture 50%	
France	73%		84%		60%		41%	
Germany	70%		84%		83%		17%	
U.K.	64%		23%		26%		11%	
Italy	49%		72%		60%		22%	
U.S.	21%		36%		51%		17%	
Japan	11%		96%		65%		13%	
Hungary	7%		19%		12%		31%	
All	42%		59%		51%		22%	

Figure 5.5 Public sector share of nonprofit revenue, by field, by country

Source: Johns Hopkins Comparative Nonprofit Sector Project

for education, Japan. In the U.K. and the U.S., the state also plays a substantial role, but a somewhat more pluralistic finding structure is also evident, with significant fee and private philanthropic support.

Conclusions and implications

The actual realities of nonprofit finance thus differ markedly from widespread conventional beliefs. While it is commonly believed that nonprofit organizations are supported chiefly by private charitable giving, in fact it is private fees and service charges that provide the largest share of total support. This is true, moreover, even in the United States, which is supposed to have the highest levels of private giving and the most highly developed private foundation sector.

As important as the role of private fees in the financial base of the nonprofit sector, however, is the role of government. In almost every service field, and in almost every country, the public sector has emerged as a major source of nonprofit finance. What is more, the public sector role appears to be growing in both scope and scale. This finding runs directly counter to one of the prevailing theories about the origins and rationale for the nonprofit sector, a theory that emphasizes the sector's role as a substitute for the state. What the data reported here suggest instead is a widespread, and growing, arena of cooperation between these two sectors. Indeed, far from substituting for the state, the nonprofit sector appears to be facilitating its expansion by assuming the task of delivering the services that government is being called on to finance. It is thus making possible the expansion of government-financed services without a corresponding expansion of the scale of the state. This system of "third-party government," long present in the American and German contexts, seems to be expanding elsewhere as well.

While this system has great advantages for both the nonprofit sector and the state, it also poses important challenges. For the state, important issues of accountability and control arise when responsibility for the delivery of state-financed services is shared with non-state entities. In addition, the state's ability to retain the support of its citizens may be attenuated when citizens can no longer see as clear a connection between the taxes they pay and the services they receive. For the nonprofit sector, the dangers are of a different sort—the potential loss of independence and the possible over-professionalization and bureaucratization of a set of organizations whose distinctiveness has sprung from their informality and responsiveness to grass-roots sentiments.

How these dangers are managed in the years ahead will importantly shape not just the future of the nonprofit sector, but also the future of the welfare state. We therefore return to these issues in Chapter 7 and explore their implications in greater detail. Before turning to these matters, however, Chapter 6 offers a more detailed sketch of the major contours of the nonprofit sector in each of our project countries.

Notes

1 The term "government payments" is used here to cover all payments made by public sector agencies for *particular services*. General income support not tied to particular services, such as general pension payments are not included, but public sector health insurance is included. This usage follows U.N. and OECD conventions, which define government, or the public sector, broadly to include all levels and branches of general, regional, and local government, *including* public agencies and corporations, social security funds, national health insurance, and similar public institutions. *Public sector payments* therefore include *grants and contracts* (i.e., direct contributions or payments by public sector organizations so defined to nonprofit organizations in support of specific activities and programs), *statutory transfers* (i.e., contributions by public agencies mandated by law to support nonprofit organizations in carrying out public purposes or satisfying entitlements), and *third-party payments* (i.e., payments made by public agencies to reimburse nonprofit organizations for services they provide to eligible individuals under social security, health insurance, or other programs). For details on the U.N. definition of the public sector, see: United Nations, *System of National Accounts 1993* (New York: United Nations, 1993), pp. 100–101, 429.

2 Also included here are earnings on assets. Both "government or public sector payments" and "private payments" can involve purchases of nonprofit services. The major difference is that with

government payments the public sector is ultimately the purchaser. It therefore seems appropriate to include such purchases with other public support to nonprofit organizations. As noted in note 1 above, this usage follows U.N. and OECD conventions.

3   See note 9, Chapter 1.

4   For a discussion of these pressures in the context of the United States, see Lester M. Salamon, "The Voluntary Sector and the Future of the Welfare State," *Nonprofit and Voluntary Sector Quarterly*, Vol. 18, No. 1 (Spring 1989), pp. 11–24. For a similar discussion in the context of the United Kingdom, see Marilyn Taylor, *Directions for the Next Decade: Understanding Social and Institutional Trends* (London: National Council on Voluntary Organizations, 1990).

5   See, for example, Organization for Economic Cooperation and Development, *The Welfare State in Crisis* (Paris: OECD, 1981); Norman Johnson, *The Welfare State in Transition: The Theory and Practice of Welfare Pluralism* (Amherst: The University of Massachusetts Press, 1987), pp. 38–40; Peter Flora, "Introduction," in Peter Flora, ed., *Growth to Limits: The Western European Welfare States Since World War II*, Vol. 1 (Berlin: Walter deGruyter, 1986), pp. x–xxix. For an examination of the implications of this rethinking for the nonprofit sector, see Lester M. Salamon, "The Rise of the Nonprofit Sector," *Foreign Affairs* (July / August 1994).

6   For a discussion of the theoretical basis for this cooperation, see Lester M. Salamon, "Of Market Failure, Government Failure, and Third-Party Government," 1987. For an analysis of the scope of this relationship in the American setting, see Lester M. Salamon, *Partners in Public Service: Government and the Nonprofit Sector in the Modern Welfare State* (Baltimore: Johns Hopkins University Press, 1994). For a comparison of the U.S. and German situations, see Lester M. Salamon and Helmut K. Anheier, "The Third Route: Subsidiarity, Third-Party Government and the Provision of Social Services in the United States and Germany," OECD, *ILE Notebook*, No. 19, 1994.

7   It is as well to remember here that these data do not include giving for sacramental religious purposes. Even if religious giving and total church income were included, however, the private share of total nonprofit income in the United States would still remain well below the government share.

8   Helmut Anheier, "An Elaborate Network: Profiling the Third Sector in Germany," in Benjamin Gidron, Ralph M. Kramer, and Lester M. Salamon, eds., *Government and the Third Sector: Emerging Relationships in Welfare States* (San Francisco: Jossey-Bass, 1992), pp. 31–56.

9   Edith Archambault, "Defining the Nonprofit Sector: France," in Lester M. Salamon and Helmut K. Anheier, eds., *Working Papers of*

the Johns Hopkins Comparative Nonprofit Sector Project, No. 7 (Baltimore: The Johns Hopkins Institute for Policy Studies, 1993), p. 21.

10 OECD, *National Income Accounts, Detailed Tables* (Paris: OECD, 1990).

11 Individuals are permitted to deduct up to 50 percent of their "adjusted gross income" in cash or ordinary property to eligible tax-exempt organizations. Slightly different limits apply to "capital-gain property," i.e., property purchased in the past that has gained in value. Corporations are permitted do deduct from their income up to 10 percent of their income. See Bruce Hopkins, *The Law of Charitable Organizations* (New York: John A. Wiley and Sons, 1987), pp. 42–43.

12 Only a narrow range of government-designated nonprofit organizations are eligible to receive tax-deductible gifts in Japan, for example. In France and Italy, the share of income that can be contributed is constrained to 5 percent and 2 percent, respectively. French law also requires governmental approval for the creation of foundations.

13 These data relate the contributions of all respondents to the personal income of all respondents, after deleting contributions to churches and religious congregations. With religious giving included, the comparable figures are 0.15 percent for France and 0.31 percent in Germany. Not included in the German figure, however, are the contributions to religion through the German "church tax," which is collected by government on behalf of the major religious denominations in Germany. Were the church tax included, the level of "giving" in Germany would rise to 1.12 percent of personal income. For further description of the surveys, see note 1, Chapter 2.

14 Computed from a Gallup survey conducted for Independent Sector. For a full report on this survey, see Virginia A. Hodgkinson and Murray Weitzman, *Giving and Volunteering in the United States* (Washington: Independent Sector, 1990), p. 41. The data reported here relate the contributions of all respondents to the income reported by the respondents after deducting reported contributions to churches and religious congregations. With the religious giving included, the comparable U.S. figure is 1.19 percent of personal income. Our estimate differs from those in Hodgkinson and Weitzman due to adjustments they have made to estimate the giving of upper-income taxpayers.

Chapter 6

COUNTRY PROFILES

While the nonprofit sector has tremendous commonalities from place to place, it also responds, as we have seen, to the peculiarities of particular national traditions and histories. Against the backdrop of the topical discussion of previous chapters, therefore, it may be useful to highlight at least some of the key features of the nonprofit sectors of each of the separate countries included in our work. To do so, we begin with the six "developed countries" (France, Germany, Italy, Japan, the United Kingdom, and the United States), then examine the one former Soviet bloc country (Hungary), and finally turn to the five "developing countries" (Brazil, Egypt, Ghana, India, and Thailand). As will become clear, although these countries differ quite substantially along a number of dimensions, they are also all experiencing, to one degree or another, what one author has termed a "global associational revolution" that is importantly transforming the relative roles of government and nonprofit organizations in virtually every part of the world.[1] The task here is to see how this general global phenomenon is playing out against the very different social, economic, political, and historical traditions of the different countries.

Developed countries

France

In France, what we have here termed the "nonprofit sector" is really part of a larger aggregation of social institutions referred to as *économie sociale,* or the "social economy." Included within this aggregation, in addition to "associations" and "foundations," which roughly correspond to our term "nonprofit sector," are cooperatives and mutuals, including large cooperative banks and mutual insurance companies.

The social economy has come to prominence in recent years as part of the government's strategy to decentralize public administration and social service delivery. It has done so, however, against the backdrop of a long French tradition of hostility toward voluntary organizations, a tradition that took root during the French Revolution, with its faith in the Rousseauean concept of the "general will" and its hostility to any institution that interposed itself between the citizen and the democratically controlled nation. Indeed, between 1791, with the passage of the Chapelier Act, and 1901, nonprofit organizations were actually illegal in France. Instead of a strong tradition of private, voluntary action, France developed a strong tradition of state-provided welfare and other services. Therefore, much of the French nonprofit sector is of relatively recent origin.[2]

Size. Against this backdrop, what is most surprising about the French nonprofit sector is that it has attained the size it has. Despite its traditional hostility to nonprofit organizations, France nonetheless belongs, together with Germany and the United Kingdom, to a middle group of countries in which the nonprofit sector represents 3–4 percent of total employment, 9–10 percent of service sector employment, and 3–5 percent of GDP. Over 800,000 people, or 4.2 percent of the entire workforce, work in the French nonprofit sector, as shown in Table 6.1. This means that employment in the French nonprofit sector exceeds the combined employment of France's two largest private employers (Alcatel-Alsthom and Générale des Eaux) by a factor of over 2 to 1! What is more, the sector has recently been one of the most dynamic in the French economy. Between 1981 and 1990, nonprofit employment increased by 40 percent while overall French employment remained fairly flat. Indeed, France has experienced a veritable explosion over the past decade in the rate at which nonprofit organizations are being created. With 31 billion ECU ($40 billion) in operating expenditures, the French nonprofit sector represents 3.3 percent of gross domestic product, a quite sizable industry.

Composition. Two subsectors, social services and education,

Table 6.1

The nonprofit sector in France

	France	7-country average
I. Employment (FTE)*		
Number	802,619	
As % of total employment	4.2%	3.4%
II. Operating expenditures		
Amount (billions)	31.3 ECU	
	39.9 US$	
As % of GDP	3.3%	3.5%
Distribution by field (%)		
Culture & recreation	17.8%	16.4%
Education & research	24.8	23.9
Health	14.5	21.4
Social services	28.9	19.5
Environment	0.7	0.8
Development & housing	6.4	5.1
Civic & advocacy	2.9	1.2
Philanthropy	0.0	0.4
International	1.1	1.3
Business, professional**	2.9	9.1
Other	0.0	0.8
Total	100%	100%
III. Revenues by major source		
As % of total		
Public sector	59.5%	43.0%
Private giving	7.1	9.5
Private fees	33.5	47.4
Total	100%	100%
* FTE = full-time equivalent	** Includes unions	

dominate the French nonprofit sector. Together, they account for about half of the sector's operating expenditures, and about 54 percent of employment. In the field of *education*, this reflects the prominent role of private Catholic schools, which, while virtually completely state-funded, have nonetheless managed to maintain their independent status. Also important has been the nonprofit role in continuing education. In the field of *social services*, the

sizable nonprofit presence is a relatively recent postwar development reinforced by the decision of the Mitterand government to
decentralize social welfare functions to local government, and
the limited capacities of local authorities to deliver the resulting
services. In fact, 58 percent of all social service jobs in France are
located in the nonprofit sector. While no general concept comparable to the German subsidiarity principle seems to be at work
here, the fact that the major conglomerates of private social service providers, UNIOPPS, *Secours Catholique*, and the socialist-
oriented *Secours Populaire*, correspond to deep-seated ideological
currents in French politics may have made it easier to legitimize
their involvement in "state" affairs.

The French nonprofit sector also includes a sizable *cultural and
recreational* component, due in large part to the popularity of
sports clubs and social tourism establishments. The share of *health*,
by contrast, is well below the seven-country average. As in the
United Kingdom and Italy, this is largely the result of a fairly
comprehensive public health system in which the public sector is
both prime funder and provider. France also has a small *philanthropic and foundation* subsector, indeed the smallest of any country in our study in proportional terms. This is due to government
regulations that have long been even more restrictive toward
foundations than toward associations—a residue of Jacobin fears
about the wealth accumulated in *ancien régime* institutions.

Revenue. In terms of its revenue structure, two characteristics
distinguish the French nonprofit sector from its counterparts elsewhere: first, its relatively high level of government support; and
second, its relatively low level of private support. With regard to
the first, France ranks second only after Germany among the
countries studied here in the share of its nonprofit income that
comes from publicly funded grants and contracts. Six out of 10
dollars of revenue represent public funds, much of it third-party
payments from social security. By contrast, only about a third is
earned income from private fees and charges. And an even smaller
7 percent comes from private giving. This reflects both the limited availability of foundation support in France and the limited
tradition of charitable giving. In a survey of French private giving,
we found that about 43 percent of the adult population donated
for charitable purposes within the previous year—well below
the 73 percent figure in the United States, but still considerable.[3]

CIVICUS
WORLD Alliance for Citiz. PAT
919 18th St NW 3rd Floor
Wash DC 20006
(202) 331-8518

Улица, дом, и проче:

Страна:

телефон:

Факс:

Электронная почта:

Сервер (Web Site):   http://

Контактный человек:

Вид Организации:

Год создания/регистрации:

Международные партнеры:

Сотрудники (сколько человек работает на Вашей орга

Описание организации:
(Пишите, пожалуйста, о
деятельности Вашей
организации, ее целях, истории,
прощедших и настоящих
программах, членстве,
публикациях и настоящих
интересах и нуждах.)

Если Ваша организация имеет эмблема или фото, которь
этом в Вашем описании и посылаете анкету с фото или эм

As a share of personal income, however, private giving was only 0.13 percent. In only one field—international assistance—did private giving provide the bulk of the revenues. Elsewhere, particularly in education and research, health, and social services, the state is the principal source of funds, reflecting a developing partnership between the state and the nonprofit sector in which the state provides the resources and nonprofit organizations deliver the services.

Current trends. Because its growth has been fueled so heavily by government support, the French nonprofit sector is particularly vulnerable to cutbacks in that support, which now seem likely. At the same time, nonprofit organizations elsewhere have proved able to resist government cutbacks, and it is reasonable to expect that similar efforts will be made in France. Beyond this, the great challenge for French nonprofit organizations is to build a more solid base of private support, not to replace the state, but to guarantee a degree of autonomy from it. For now, however, what is most striking is what a significant force the French nonprofit sector, even in the restricted way we have defined it, has become.

Germany

Compared to the situation in France, the nonprofit sector in Germany is much more highly institutionalized and integrated into the fabric of the German social welfare system. Reflecting a rich tradition of subsidiarity, self-governance, and decentralization, the nonprofit sector has long since taken its place as a major presence in German society, even though its precise scale and contours have never been charted with care. At the same time, the sector has grown massively in recent years and faces new challenges in the light of reunification and the strain of coping with more slowly growing public funding.

Size. As shown in Table 6.2, the West German nonprofit sector is a $54 billion (42 billion ECU) economy that employs slightly over 1 million full-time equivalent employees, or about 3.7 percent of the German workforce. One out of every 10 German service workers is employed in the nonprofit sector. In fact, the nonprofit sector employs four times as many workers as Volkswagen, the country's largest employer, and twice as many as Volkswagen and Daimler-Benz combined.

Table 6.2

The nonprofit sector in Germany

	Germany	7-country average
I. Employment (FTE)*		
Total nonprofit employees (FTE)*	1,017,945	
As % of total employment	3.7%	3.4%
II. Operating expenditures		
Amount (billions)	42.3 ECU	
	53.9 US$	
As % of GDP	3.6%	3.5%
Distribution by field in %		
Culture & recreation	7.3%	16.4%
Education & research	11.9	23.9
Health	34.5	21.4
Social services	23.1	19.5
Environment	0.7	0.8
Development & housing	14.8	5.1
Civic & advocacy	1.1	1.2
Philanthropy	0.2	0.4
International	1.5	1.3
Business, professional**	5.3	9.1
Other	0.0	0.8
Total	100%	100%
III. Revenues by major source		
As % of total		
Public sector	68.2%	43.0%
Private giving	3.9	9.5
Private fees	27.9	47.4
Total	100%	100%
* FTE = full-time equivalent	** Includes unions	

Though firmly established in Germany by the early 1960s, the nonprofit sector has nevertheless grown rapidly in recent decades. In fact, in proportional terms, employment in the nonprofit sector in Germany has grown faster between 1970 and 1990 than employment in any other sector, including manufacturing and services. Between 1980 and 1990 alone, the nonprofit sector contributed one out of every nine jobs added to the German economy. The bulk of these increases occurred in the fields of health and social services, which, not accidentally, were the areas of greatest governmental expansion. In other words, as the Christian Democratic and Social Democratic coalitions of the 1970s and 1980s built a modern welfare state, they simultaneously built the German nonprofit sector.

In eastern Germany, very different forces are at work. Here, as in the west, the nonprofit sector has outperformed other parts of the economy in terms of job creation. In fact, the nonprofit sector seems to be the only sector other than finance and insurance that added any significant number of jobs at all, increasing the sector's employment from 86,000 in 1990 to 92,000 in early 1992, while overall employment declined from 7.6 to 6.9 million. However, this expansion is largely the result of employment policies that created so-called ABM jobs (Arbeitsbeschaffungsmaßnahmen) as an alternative to unemployment. Largely funded by the public sector, many ABM jobs are located in the health, social services, and education fields.

Composition and growth. Six large "free welfare associations" dominate the German nonprofit sector, as noted in Chapter 4. These associations represent nonprofit organizations grouped around religious (Catholic, Protestant, and Jewish), class (worker), or interest (Red Cross, unaffiliated) lines. Reflecting this, nonprofit organizations are particularly prominent in two fields in Germany: health and social services. Together, they account for two out of every three jobs in the German nonprofit sector, and nearly six out of every 10 dollars in operating expenditures. Within the health field, nonprofit organizations represent 34 percent of all jobs; and within the social service field the comparable figure is 61 percent. This is so because these are the two fields in which the doctrine of subsidiarity, which obliges the state to defer to voluntary institutions wherever possible, is most powerfully in force. By contrast, subsidiarity is less prominent in the fields of culture and recreation, and education and research, and the nonprofit sector in Germany is correspondingly less highly developed in those spheres. In fact, were it not for its prominent role in the fields of health and social services, the German nonprofit sector would rank among the smallest in our study, both in absolute and relative terms. In other words, the principle of subsidiarity serves as the economic bedrock for the German nonprofit sector. It spells out a partnership between the state and the nonprofit sector, and where this partnership developed, the nonprofit sector grew into a sizable economic and social force; where it did not develop, the nonprofit sector remained much less significant.

Revenue. Reflecting this fact, the German nonprofit sector has the highest proportion of public sector funding of any of the countries in our study. Nearly seven out of every 10 dollars of nonprofit revenue derive from public funds, half of which come in the form of third-party payments from social security and public health insurance schemes. By contrast, the share of nonprofit revenue that comes from private charitable contributions is the lowest for any country except Japan. This is consistent with the results of a survey we conducted of giving and volunteering in Germany, which revealed that only 0.18 percent of personal income finds its way into nonreligious charitable contributions. To this must be added, of course, the semi-voluntary "church tax," which the state collects on behalf of the major religious denominations. However, most of this goes for the salary of church personnel as well as the maintenance of church property, and the contributions are not wholly voluntary. German nonprofit organizations also receive a disproportionately small share of their income from fees and charges (28 percent vs. the seven-country average of 47 percent). Fee income is considerably more important, however, in the fields of culture and recreation, environment, and housing, where government is less active. What this suggests is that if public sector support declines, German nonprofit organizations are likely to turn increasingly toward the market for support, unless significant changes can be made in the levels of private philanthropic support.

Key trends. The current policy debate in Germany is dominated by the social and political challenges of unification. The Unity Treaty stated that "the establishment and expansion of the Free Welfare Associations . . . will be supported [by the state] in the context of constitutional responsibilities." Since then, with substantial public funds, the welfare associations have expanded into eastern Germany and built up a network of organizations in an effort to meet the growing and shifting demands for social and health services. In contrast to western Germany, where

Catholics and Protestants make up close to 85 percent of the population, only about one-third of eastern Germans are members of a church. This puts limits on the strong policy connection between established religion and the subsidiarity principle. Given a continued strain on public budgets, the process of unification will most likely result in greater flexibility in how the subsidiarity principle is applied, combined with greater roles allocated to other providers. In the process, however, it seems likely that the German nonprofit sector will experience a process of "marketization" not unlike that evident in the United States.[4]

Italy

Ambiguity is the term that probably best captures the position of the nonprofit sector in Italy. Italian nonprofit organizations have long operated in a "no-man's land" between a suspicious state bureaucracy and a resistant Church apparatus.[5] After trying throughout much of the latter 19th century to subjugate the Church and its array of social institutions, the state essentially reached a modus vivendi in the early 20th century under which the Church agreed to make its institutions formally part of the public sector, while the state agreed to let the Church operate these institutions pretty much as before. The Italian nonprofit sector thus largely disappeared in formal terms while its institutions continued to grow. During more recent times, efforts have been made to clarify this ambiguous status as more secular institutions have emerged and a more explicit partnership was forged between the nonprofit sector and the state.

Size. Perhaps because of its ambiguous legal status, the nonprofit sector in Italy appears to be much smaller than its counterparts elsewhere in Europe. Even so, Italian nonprofits employ over 400,000 workers, three times the number employed at Fiat, the country's largest private sector firm. In terms of operating expenditures, the sector represents a $22 billion economy (17 billion ECU), or 2 percent of GDP (see Table 6.3).

Composition. Social service activities, and education and research, dominate the Italian nonprofit sector, with nearly two-thirds (64 percent) of total nonprofit employment and nearly half of total operating expenditures. The presence in social services reflects the growth of local government funding of nonprofit social

Table 6.3

The nonprofit sector in Italy

	Italy	7-country average
I. Employment (FTE)*		
Number	416,383	
As % of total employment	1.8%	3.4%
II. Operating expenditures		
Amount (billions)	17.1 ECU	
	21.8 US$	
As % of GDP	2.0%	3.5%
Distribution by field in %		
Culture & recreation	8.5%	16.4%
Education & research	21.7	23.9
Health	16.4	21.4
Social services	24.9	19.5
Environment	0.2	0.8
Development & housing	1.7	5.1
Civic & advocacy	2.2	1.2
Philanthropy	1.0	0.4
International	1.3	1.3
Business, professional**	22.9	9.1
Other	0.0	0.8
Total	100%	100%
III. Revenues by major source		
As % of total		
Public sector	42.6%	43.0%
Private giving	4.1	9.5
Private fees	53.2	47.4
Total	100%	100%
* FTE = full-time equivalent	** Includes unions	

service activities. The latter is a legacy of religiously affiliated primary and secondary education. Also notable is the prominent role of business, professional, and labor organizations within the Italian nonprofit sector. As the country with one of the highest unionization rates in the European Union, Italy provides considerable public support for union activities and has developed a significant institutional space for the representation of private economic interest and for the involvement of professional organizations in service provision, vocational training, and licensing. By contrast, only limited nonprofit involvement is evident in the fields of culture, health, or housing, where government service provision is extensive. In fact, the absence of a substantial nonprofit presence in the country's health sector accounts for much of the overall smaller scale of the nonprofit sector in Italy.[6]

Revenue. Next to the United Kingdom, Italy's nonprofit sector is the most "commercial" among the European Union countries in our study. Private earnings account for over half of the revenues of Italian nonprofit organizations. By comparison, private donative income is an extremely meager 4 percent and government support only 43 percent. Private fee income is particularly important in the fields of culture and recreation, education, environment, and the unusually large Italian business and professional association subsector, which naturally receives most of its funds from dues and fees. By contrast, the more "normal" European pattern of extensive governmental support to nonprofit organizations is evident in the social service field.

Key trends. While private organizations have historically played a relatively limited role in Italy's highly centralized social welfare system, recent changes have begun to alter this. Most notably, a major decentralization law in 1977 vested important new powers in local governments. Since these governments have lacked the institutional capacities to deliver human services themselves, they have turned extensively to nonprofit organizations for help. At the same time, steps have been taken to clarify the legal position of nonprofit organizations. Thus, the old Church affiliated *Opere Pie*, which were formally nationalized while remaining administratively part of the Church, have now been given the right to reconstitute themselves as private institutions. Similarly, Law 280 of 1990 is changing the status of Italian public banks. Under the new legislation, banks are encouraged to set up foundations that will hold the banks' shares and draw on the resulting dividends to support publicly oriented or charitable activities. Nevertheless, the ambiguity that has long characterized the Italian nonprofit sector still persists, impeding full development of this sector as a meaningful social force.

Japan

Japan is in many senses the most restrictive of the developed countries in terms of the ease or difficulty of forming nonprofit organizations. No all-encompassing legal structure is available for the chartering of what we have referred to here as nonprofit organizations. The closest Japanese law comes to such a concept is the *Kōeki hōjin*, or charitable organization. A wide variety of types of nonprofit organizations is eligible for registration as *kōeki hōjin*. However, such registration is exceedingly difficult, requiring the approval of the "competent governmental agency" in the field in which the organization hopes to operate and the availability of substantial financial assets (300 million yen, or $2.3 million, in the case of organizations approved by the Ministry of Foreign Affairs, for example). Because most ministries have passed their own laws stipulating the kinds of nonprofit organizations they will authorize, moreover, most organizations simply seek registration under these separate provisions since this is the route the "competent government agency" prefers. Although a sizable nonprofit sector exists, therefore, it is chopped up into a number of discrete subsectors by a set of field-specific laws permitting the formation of not-for-profit institutions only to perform relatively narrowly defined functions, and even then only with the permission of the designated governmental ministry.[7] No concept of an independent, private voluntary sector existing apart from, and to some extent in opposition to, the state consequently exists in Japan, though such a concept is beginning to emerge.

Size. Reflecting the limitations under which it operates, the nonprofit sector in Japan has remained small, at least in relative terms. Thus, nonprofit organizations, as we have defined them here, represent only 2.5 percent of total employment, and about 3.2 percent of gross domestic product, in Japan, as shown in Table 6.4.

It must not be thought, however, that nonprofit organizations are consequently an insignificant presence in Japanese society. For one thing, because of the scale of the Japanese economy, even these small percentages translate into a set of institutions with considerable economic weight. Thus, as we have seen, the relatively small Japanese nonprofit sector nevertheless employs more people than its counterparts in Germany, France, Italy, and

Table 6.4

The nonprofit sector in Japan

	Japan	7-country average
I. Employment (FTE)*		
Number	1,440,228	
As % of total employment	2.5%	3.4%
II. Operating expenditures		
Amount (billions)	74.7 ECU	
	94.1 US$	
As % of GDP	3.2%	3.5%
Distribution by field in %		
Culture & recreation	1.2%	16.4%
Education & research	39.5	23.9
Health	27.7	21.4
Social services	13.8	19.5
Environment	0.2	0.8
Development & housing	0.3	5.1
Civic & advocacy	0.9	1.2
Philanthropy	0.1	0.4
International	0.5	1.3
Business, professional**	11.4	9.1
Other	4.5	0.8
Total	100%	100%
III. Revenues by major source		
As % of total		
Public sector	38.3%	43.0%
Private giving	1.3	9.5
Private fees	60.4	47.4
Total	100%	100%
* FTE = full-time equivalent	** Includes unions	

the U.K. Put somewhat differently, Japanese nonprofit organizations employ more than three times as many people as Japan's two largest private employers, Hitachi and Toshiba.

Composition. Education and research and health are by far the dominant fields of nonprofit action in Japan, accounting together for two-thirds of all nonprofit expenditures. Most Japanese universities and a significant minority of its elementary and secondary schools are nonprofit in form, though they are subject to fairly stringent governmental regulations on curricular and related matters. Nonprofit organizations are also active in the field of scientific research. A similar situation exists in the health sector, where some 7,000 *iryō hōjin*, or health corporations, dominate the delivery of health care through hospitals, clinics, and related facilities. Nonprofit organizations are also active in the social service field, though here they play a more supplemental role, buttressing state-provided aid in certain narrowly defined areas, such as residential care for the elderly and day care for children under five. The specialized social welfare corporations (*shakaifukushi hōjin*) active in this field therefore operate as quasigovernmental corporations. Finally, about 11 percent of all nonprofit expenditures in Japan are made by a variety of business and professional organizations and alumni associations.

Outside of these fields, nonprofit activity is relatively limited in Japan. Thus, there is little nonprofit activity in the fields of culture or recreation, environmental protection, housing, or civic affairs. As a general rule, where it has been in the interest of government agencies to permit the creation of nonprofit organizations, such organizations have come into existence. Where government policy has seen little use for nonprofit organizations, such organizations have not been either encouraged or permitted.

Revenue. Although government has been crucial in opening the way to the creation of nonprofit organizations in Japan, it has not been the principal source of financial support. Rather, 60 percent of nonprofit revenue in Japan comes from private fees and charges, the highest of any country we examined. For the most part, this represents tuition receipts for private universities and schools. Close to 90 percent of the income of this important element of the Japanese nonprofit sector takes this form.

Outside of the education field, government support is far more important. Thus the two other significant components of the Japanese nonprofit sector—health and social services—receive most of their income from the public sector. For example, 96 percent of the income of the substantial nonprofit medical corporations originates with government, as does 65 percent of the income of the social service corporations. Private giving, by contrast, is virtually nonexistent in Japan. Only 1 percent of nonprofit income overall originates with private charitable contributions. One reason for this may be the limited tax incentives for charitable contributions. Donations to only one very narrow category of organizations, the so-called *tokutei kōeki zōshin hōjin*, or "special public-interest-promoting organizations," are eligible for such deductions.

Current trends. The key issue for the future of the nonprofit sector in Japan is whether the prevailing relatively rigid system of state control will survive or be replaced by a more flexible and open system more conducive to the formation of nonprofit organizations. The general opening of Japanese society and the emergence of new social problems and tensions resulting from the aging of the population and growing hostility to rigid social controls make it likely that people will turn increasingly to organized voluntary activity through which to express competing points of view. Whether the government will accept a truly collaborative relationship with a more independent nonprofit sector, however, is still very much open to question.

United Kingdom

The nonprofit sector has a rich and varied history in the United Kingdom, stretching back at least to the Elizabethan Statute of Charitable Uses of 1601 and embracing 18th- and 19th-century social welfare agencies, such as Dr. Barnardo's, 19th-century "friendly societies" and "building societies" formed to protect disadvantaged industrial workers, as well as more recent advocacy organizations in such fields as environmental protection, world peace, and women's rights. The emergence of such organizations has been governed less by any legislative enactment than by the common law premise of an inherent right to associate together for the public good. Because the status of being a "charitable" organization now brings with it important tax and legal privileges, England and Wales established a quasi-independent Charity Commission that reviews organization by-laws and related documents to determine which organizations qualify. In carrying out its mission, the Commission is guided by an exceedingly complex and ever-changing body of case law that defines, and redefines, the meaning of "charitableness" for each era.[8] What is more, the structure and role of the U.K. nonprofit sector has been importantly shaped by the content of government social policy, which relegated this sector to a relatively limited role in much of the postwar period, but has since thrust it into unaccustomed prominence over the past decade.

Size. Reflecting its rich history, the nonprofit sector is a rather sizable presence in the U.K., despite the dramatic growth of state-provided social welfare services in the immediate aftermath of World War II. Thus, close to 1 million people work in the U.K. "voluntary" sector, about 4 percent of all U.K. workers, as shown in Table 6.5. This is nearly five times more jobs than are provided by the U.K.'s largest private employer, Unilever. In addition, an estimated 51 percent of the U.K. population is involved in formal volunteer activities. In expenditure terms, the U.K. nonprofit sector is a $47 billion (37 billion ECU) economy, the equivalent of 4.8 percent of GDP. This makes the U.K. nonprofit sector the second largest after the U.S. as a share of gross domestic product.

Composition. Nonprofit organizations are especially active in three fields in the U.K.: education, culture and recreation, and social services. Education alone absorbs 42 percent of all nonprofit expenditures. This reflects the long tradition of British "public schools," the historic presence of a sizable independent university sector, and the recent transformation of formerly local-government-run colleges and polytechnics into private colleges.

Another 21 percent of U.K. nonprofit expenditures goes for culture and recreation, much of it for social and recreation clubs and sports activities. Nonprofit organizations are also active in the field of social services, where they perform both an advocacy and service-delivery function. Finally, nonprofit organizations play a distinctive role in the U.K. in carrying out international assistance activities and in housing, the latter a by-product of a rich history of housing societies and housing associations for the working class. More generally, nonprofit organizations have functioned as a base for a wide variety of social movements, both historically and at the present time.

One area where nonprofit organizations are noticeably underrepresented in the U.K. is health. Because of the creation of the National Health Service after World War II, many private nonprofit hospitals were converted to public ownership. Were it

Table 6.5

The nonprofit sector in the United Kingdom

	U.K.	7-country average
I. Employment (FTE)*		
Number	945,883	
As % of total employment	4.0%	3.4%
II. Operating expenditures		
Amount (billions)	36.9 ECU	
	47.0 US$	
As % of GDP	4.8%	3.5%
Distribution by field in %		
Culture & recreation	20.5%	16.4%
Education & research	42.4	23.9
Health	3.5	21.4
Social services	11.5	19.5
Environment	2.2	0.8
Development & housing	7.8	5.1
Civic & advocacy	0.7	1.2
Philanthropy	0.7	0.4
International	3.7	1.3
Business, professional**	7.0	9.1
Other	0.0	0.8
Total	100%	100%
III. Revenues by major source		
As % of total		
Public sector	39.8%	43.0%
Private giving	12.1	9.5
Private fees	48.2	47.4
Total	100%	100%
* FTE = full-time equivalent	** Includes unions	

not for this fact, the U.K. nonprofit sector would probably out-distance the American in relative size.

Revenue. Perhaps the distinctive feature of the revenue base of the U.K. nonprofit sector is its balance. No single source dominates the sector's finances. Although fee income is the largest single source, it accounts for slightly less than half of all revenue, and much of this is concentrated in the fields of recreation and business and professional activity. Interestingly, in the education sphere, although most of the institutions are private, close to two-thirds of the revenue is public. An interesting compromise has consequently been struck in the educational field in which government provides the support to allow citizens to attend university, but permits the universities to function as private, nonprofit institutions. A similar partnership appears to be emerging in the social service field, though here private charitable donations are more important. More generally, the U.K. nonprofit sector retains a significant level of private charitable support, amounting to 12 percent of income overall, but representing between 25 percent and 40 percent of income in such fields as health, environment, and social services.

Key issues. Perhaps the key issue affecting the future of the U.K. nonprofit sector is the evolution of its relationship with the state. After an extended period of welfare state expansion in the U.K., the conservative regime of Margaret Thatcher sought to shift more of societal problem-solving onto the shoulders of the private sector, including private voluntary organizations. Significant changes are consequently being made in the provision of community care and in the structure of the health system. While many of these changes augur well for the nonprofit sector, others are more problematic, such as the shift from a system of outright grants for nonprofit providers to a system of purchase-of-service contracts that may subject providers to closer governmental scrutiny. As the scope of governmental support increases, moreover, U.K. nonprofit organizations will need to buttress their private support as well in order to retain a meaningful degree of independent financing.

United States

The United States has clearly the largest nonprofit sector, in both absolute and relative terms, of any of the countries considered here. However, it is also one of the most frequently misunderstood. Reliance on the nonprofit sector reflects a long-standing American pattern of individualism and hostility to government. The American tradition of reliance on the nonprofit sector has thus been the other side of a set of social policies that has kept governmental social welfare protections rather limited. Indeed, support for philanthropy and nonprofit organizations has frequently been used to justify opposition to the extension of public social welfare protections, thus thrusting the nonprofit sector into the middle of an essentially ideological dispute that portrays these two sectors as fundamental antagonists. In fact, however, despite this rhetoric, an elaborate pattern of government-nonprofit cooperation has developed in the United States, combining the resource-raising capabilities of the state with the service-delivering capabilities of private nonprofit organizations. In addition, the nonprofit sector has functioned, particularly since the 1960s, as the seedbed for a host of crucial social movements that have animated American political life over the past three decades, including the civil rights movement, the environmental movement, the consumer movement, the gay rights movement, the women's movement, and many more.

American law identifies 26 types of tax-exempt nonprofit organizations. Except for business and professional associations, most of those embraced by the definition of the nonprofit sector used here fall under one subsection of the revenue code, section 501 (c) (3), which covers organizations engaged in scientific, educational, charitable, and related purposes. These organizations are not only exempt from most federal and local taxes on their own income (except for unrelated business income), but also are eligible to receive tax-deductible contributions, i.e., charitable contributions that the donors, whether individuals or corporations, can deduct from their own income in computing their tax liabilities. Confirmation of 501 (c) (3) status is provided by the Internal Revenue Service upon review of an organization's by-laws and statement of purpose and is fairly routine.

Size. The nonprofit sector as defined here is a $346 billion "industry" in the United States, employing over 7 million people, as shown in Table 6.6. This means that the sector represents over 6 percent of the gross domestic product and employs close to 7 percent of the country's labor force. Put somewhat differently, there are 10 times as many people employed in America's nonprofit sector as in its largest private company, General Motors.

Composition. The size of the American nonprofit sector is a bit deceptive, however, because three-quarters of its expenditures are made by two types of organizations: hospitals and higher

Table 6.6

The nonprofit sector in the United States

	U.S.	7-country average
I. Employment (FTE)*		
Number	7,130,823	
As % of total employment	6.9%	3.4%
II. Operating expenditures		
Amount (billions)	272.0 ECU	
	346.4 US$	
As % of GDP	6.3%	3.5%
Distribution by field in %		
Culture & recreation	3.1%	16.4%
Education & research	22.7	23.9
Health	52.6	21.4
Social services	9.9	19.5
Environment	0.7	0.8
Development & housing	3.1	5.1
Civic & advocacy	0.3	1.2
Philanthropy	0.4	0.4
International	1.2	1.3
Business, professional**	5.1	9.1
Other	0.9	0.8
Total	100%	100%
III. Revenues by major source		
As % of total		
Public sector	29.6%	43.0%
Private giving	18.7	9.5
Private fees	51.8	47.4
Total	100%	100%
* FTE = full-time equivalent	** Includes unions	

education institutions.[9] Hospitals and other health care providers alone account for over 50 percent of the nonprofit sector's expenditures in the United States. This reflects the fact that America's health system is largely private nonprofit in structure. Just over half of all hospitals are private-nonprofit in form. About one-third are governmental. And the balance (about 17 percent) are for-profit.

Nonprofit organizations are also quite prevalent in the higher education field in the United States. About half of all colleges and universities are nonprofit, though they enroll a considerably smaller share of the total students. Overall, education absorbs about one-fourth of all nonprofit expenditures. By contrast, a considerably smaller 10 percent of all nonprofit expenditures are made in the area of social services. However, this understates the importance of the nonprofit role in this field. Almost 60 percent of all social service providers are nonprofit organizations. These organizations offer child day care, counseling, information and referral services, family services, adoption assistance, and a host of similar activities. Similarly, although only 3 percent of all nonprofit expenditures go into culture and recreation, the nonprofit role in this field too is considerable. Thus, most of the symphonies, art galleries, operas, and museums in the country are nonprofit in basic structure.

Revenues. Contrary to widespread beliefs, private philanthropy is not the major source of nonprofit revenue in the United States. Rather, over half of this revenue comes from private fees. Most of this takes the form of tuition payments to private universities and private insurance and patient payments for health care. Another 30 percent of nonprofit income comes from government. The largest portion of this comes in the form of reimbursements for medical costs under the country's government-funded health insurance for the elderly and the indigent. The balance takes the form either of grants or grants connected to purchase-of-service contracts. Only 19 percent of total nonprofit revenue comes from private giving. Of this, the largest share takes the form of individual giving, either directly or through federated fundraising organizations such as United Way or the American Cancer Society. About 20 percent of private giving comes from endowed foundations and corporations, roughly half from each.

In some fields, of course, these proportions are quite different. Thus, fees are far more important in the fields of health care, education, and culture. Government and private giving, by contrast, are more important in the fields of social services and civic life.

Key issues. The decade of the 1980s was a stressful one for American nonprofit organizations. On the one hand, these organizations were showered with government attention. On the other hand, they lost significant portions of their government support as a conservative political regime sought to reduce government spending and shift a greater share of the burden for coping with social needs onto private philanthropic sources. At the same time, changing social mores, the continued growth of female labor force participation, and the expansion of the elderly population translated into new demands for the services that nonprofit organizations provide. In response, nonprofit organizations successfully oriented themselves toward the growing markets for their services, boosting their earned incomes substantially. As they did so, however, they encountered growing competition from for-profit businesses entering the same fields. The resulting "marketization" of welfare has come to be the prevailing reality of nonprofit operations in a context of stable or slowly growing government support and limited expansion of private, charitable income.

Former Communist Bloc

Hungary

Despite a rich late-19th- and early-20th-century history, the nonprofit sector in Hungary essentially did not exist as of the mid-1980s, except for hobby clubs and the so-called "social organizations" that were largely part of the state-socialist system.[10] This changed, first gradually and then more dramatically, when, in 1989, a law on associations was passed. Since then, the Hungarian nonprofit sector has undergone rapid development and passed through a series of significant legal and policy changes intended to clarify the position and role of this sector in the new Hungary.

Size. Compared to the developed market economies, the Hungarian nonprofit sector is understandably still small, with 33,000 employees as of 1990, or 0.8 percent of total employment. In terms of expenditure, it represents a $0.4 billion economy (.31 billion ECU), or 1.2 percent of Hungary's GDP. However, when we take into account that in 1991–1992 most of this sector was less than perhaps one or two years old, we begin to fathom the dynamism of the situation. Indeed, as of 1990, Hungary boasted

Table 6.7

The nonprofit sector in Hungary

	Hungary	7-country average
I. Employment (FTE)*		
Number	32,738	
As % of total employment	0.8%	3.4%
II. Operating expenditures		
Amount (billions)	0.31 ECU	
	0.4 US$	
As % of GDP	1.2%	3.5%
Distribution by field in %		
Culture & recreation	56.2%	16.4%
Education & research	4.0	23.9
Health	0.9	21.4
Social services	24.9	19.5
Environment	1.5	0.8
Development & housing	1.4	5.1
Civic & advocacy	0.4	1.2
Philanthropy	0.7	0.4
International	0.1	1.3
Business, professional**	9.4	9.1
Other	0.5	0.8
Total	100%	100%
III. Revenues by major source		
As % of total		
Public sector	23.3%	43.0%
Private giving	19.7	9.5
Private fees	57.0	47.4
Total	100%	100%
* FTE = full-time equivalent	** Includes unions	

13,000 nonprofit organizations. Three years later, in 1993, this had grown to over 36,000.

Composition. The composition of the Hungarian nonprofit sector is very much in transition. In terms of expenditures, the field of culture and recreation is clearly dominant, reflecting the shifting of resources from the cultural ministries to foundations in the last two years of Communist rule as well as the continued presence of sports, hobby, and recreational associations that had been tolerated under state socialism. More recently, however, nonprofit organizations have become more active in other fields, particularly education and research, and social services.

Revenue. Unlike eastern Germany, where a massive influx of public funds has underwritten the expansion of nonprofit organizations, in Hungary nonprofit organizations have been forced to rely chiefly on earned income, much of it from enterprises that the organizations operate. Fifty-seven percent of total nonprofit revenue in Hungary comes from this source. By contrast, only about two out of 10 dollars come from the public sector. Moreover, the share of income coming from private giving in Hungary is the highest among our project countries, surpassing the proportions in the United States and the United Kingdom.

Current trends. Two key developments are currently shaping the evolution of the nonprofit sector in Hungary. The first is a backlash against a series of disclosures of abuse of the foundation form to shield new business ventures from taxation. These abuses, an unfortunate by-product of the early effort to liberalize Communist-era laws prohibiting the formation of foundations, have given the nonprofit field a bad name in Hungary almost before it got established. In response, a variety of the much more restrictive laws have been passed. The second important development was the passage of new legislation in the social welfare field authorizing national and local governments to contract with nonprofit organizations to deliver publicly financed social services. Depending on the reaction of these authorities and the speed with which nonprofit organizations develop solid capabilities, this legislation could open to nonprofits in Hungary the same opportunities for growth that the comparable provisions have created in Germany and France.

Developing countries

Compared to the more developed countries, the nonprofit sector in the developing countries is typically considerably more complex and diverse, but also far less well understood. According to popular stereotypes in the West, philanthropy is essentially a

Western phenomenon associated with the Judeo-Christian tradition and therefore far less prominent in other cultures or religious traditions. In fact, however, rich philanthropic traditions are evident in virtually every major religious culture—in the Islamic concept of *Zakat*, in the emphasis on voluntarism in precolonial India, in the charitable culture of the Buddhist monasteries, and in the Akan culture of western Africa. The emergence of Western nonprofit organizations has thus come on top of a rich overlay of voluntary institutions in most developing countries—traditional tribal or religious groupings, Western missionary associations created during the colonial era, modern professional associations, and more recent NGOs, or nongovernmental organizations, engaged in relief and development work.

Brazil

Size and scope. Brazil typifies this complex pattern, with long-established nonprofit organizations such as exclusive private schools, large-scale nonprofit hospitals, and professional associations coexisting with numerous nonregistered community associations and advocacy groups.[11] As of 1990, close to 200,000 nonprofit entities were registered with the Federal Revenue Bureau in Brasilia. This included 11,076 foundations (almost exclusively operating foundations) and 179,010 associations. Over one-quarter of these organizations were located either in São Paolo or Rio de Janeiro.

In terms of areas of activity, we found that:
- 29 percent work primarily in social services and health;
- 23 percent represent sport and recreational groups;
- 19 percent provide cultural and educational services;
- 9 percent are business and professional associations and unions; and
- 20 percent operate as multipurpose organizations.

Other data reveal that 16 percent of Brazil's 38,000 health establishments are nonprofit organizations, as are 35 percent of the 77 hospitals with over 500 beds. Nonprofit libraries represent about 20 percent of the 22,000 libraries operating in the country, and nonprofit museums represent a third of all Brazilian museums. Information on the field of education is very sketchy; however, 28 of the country's universities are nonprofit, and the Catholic

Church maintains a wide network of primary and secondary schools. Beyond this are literally thousands of unregistered community organizations in poor urban and rural areas, which seem to have mushroomed in the last decade as a result of deepening economic and political problems.

Recent growth. Brazil's nonprofit sector has expanded significantly in recent years. Between 1978 and 1991, the number of organizations registered with the Federal Revenue Bureau increased from 76,000 to 190,000, or by close to 9,000 per year on average. Data collected by Santos show that the typical number of associations registered in the state of Rio de Janeiro per annum jumped from 743 for the 1950s to 1,233 for the 1970s to 2,500 for the first half of the 1980s alone.[12] Figures for São Paolo show very similar trends.

Revenue. Little is known about the revenues of Brazilian nonprofit organizations. With the help of a sample survey of nonprofit organizations in Rio de Janeiro, however, we were able to gain some initial insight based on returns of 140 nonprofit organizations. What is most striking about the results is the pronounced share of private fees (55 percent) in total revenue, whereas government sources contribute only 7 percent, and private donations 6 percent. Support from international agencies accounts for 8 percent of income, and the remaining 25 percent comes from transfers from parent organizations like the Catholic Church. While our sample included many larger nonprofit organizations active in social services and community development, smaller community groups may well have been underrepresented. Nonetheless, our results seem to suggest that the nonprofit sector in developing countries like Brazil, with a diverse economy and a small, though influential, urban middle class, is less dependent on public and international funds than is often assumed.

Egypt

Egypt's nonprofit sector likewise represents a rich mixture of institutional types—Islamic, Coptic, and Western. As in other Middle Eastern countries, nonprofit activities have a long history in Egypt, reflecting the traditional Islamic system of *Al Waqf*, or charitable bequests, as well as the Islamic concept of *Al Zakat*, or alms giving, which mandates that 2.5 percent of income be given to charity each year.[13]

Though rooted in these traditional concepts, however, the Egyptian nonprofit sector has expanded considerably in recent years, albeit at a rate that lags somewhat behind that in other developing countries. One reason for this may be the continued distrust of the nonprofit sector on the part of the state, a distrust born in part of the Nasser Government's concern about the use of nonprofit organizations by radical Islamic groups to mobilize mass support against the modernizing reforms of the new regime. To prevent this, Egypt adopted a restrictive law in 1964 to control the spread of nonprofit organizations. This Law 32 gives the state the power to object to the establishment of nonprofit organizations on broad national security grounds, so as to prevent, among others, the revival of previously dissolved organizations like the Islamic Brothers Associations, which nevertheless remains the strongest informal association in Egypt. Moreover, once established, the Ministry of Social Affairs can assume wide-ranging powers in the management and governance of associations. The government has also extended its reach to the traditional *Al Waqf* institutions, establishing a Ministry of *Al Waqf* with powers to oversee the allocation of religiously inspired charitable bequests and nationalizing Islamic and Coptic hospitals in 1960. In addition, through the public Nasser Bank for Social Work, the government pools donations made at thousands of individual mosques throughout the country for development and relief purposes, injecting the state into the relations between citizens and their mosques.

Scope and structure. Despite this restrictive and highly politicized environment, the nonprofit sector has still managed to assume a rather significant role in Egypt, particularly since the adoption in 1974 of more liberal economic policies and the acceptance of a multiparty political system. As of 1990, 19,348 nonprofit organizations were identified by the Ministry of Development. Based on a survey conducted for this project:

- about one-quarter (27 percent) of the organizations are cultural and scientific associations;
- almost half (45 percent) work in the field of social services, which includes family services, general social assistance, and services for the elderly; and
- another quarter (27 percent) are active in community development.

In addition, there are several large and influential professional

associations in Egypt. Together, they have a combined membership of over 1 million. In the absence of a full democratic order,
these associations have become an important vehicle for the country's middle class to take part in the economic and political affairs
of the country.

Revenue. Little information is available on the revenue structure of Egyptian nonprofit organizations. However, our data seem
to suggest that foreign aid appears to account for significant
proportions of total revenues, whereas government funds seem
to play a lesser role. At the same time, almost a third of the staff
of certain ministries, such as the Ministry of Social Welfare, are
essentially seconded to work at nonprofit organizations.

Key trends. Largely because of the political situation in the
country, the growth rate of Egypt's nonprofit sector has been
somewhat subdued. Between 1985 and 1990, the number of associations under the tutelage of the Ministry of Social Affairs
increased by about 2 percent each year. However, these data fail
to capture what appears to be a much more rapid rate of growth
on the part of informal and unregistered Islamic associations.
These organizations, a manifestation of what has come to be
called "popular Islam," have created a virtual second society to
supply education and health services that the state, with its
dwindling resources, has been unable to provide. In the process,
they are building the political power of the Islamic movement
and effectively supplanting the state as the source of social and
educational services.

Ghana

The nonprofit sector in Ghana also reflects the institutional diversity typical of developing countries, with the simultaneous
presence of elements of African, Western, and Islamic cultures.
The country's nonprofit sector may be classified into four main
categories:

- *Indigenous associations and self-help societies* such as *susu*, a widespread form of informal credit and savings association, or the
  so-called *Asafo Company*, which provides a variety of mutual
  support services;
- *Church-related charitable organizations* such as the Christian
  Rehabilitation Foundation, or the Muslim Koran Study Asso-

ciation. Many of these organizations date back to the colonial period and are offsprings of missionary societies that founded hospitals, schools, and orphanages;

- *Nongovernmental organizations* (NGOs), which include a broad array of both indigenous and international organizations engaged in a wide assortment of development activities, from providing rural health care to assisting small enterprise development. Examples include the May Day Rural Health Clinic, the Ghana Local Reconstruction Movement, AFRICARE, Technoserve, and the Adventist Relief and Development Agency. These organizations have recently come together to form the Ghana Association of Private Voluntary Organizations in Development (GAPVOD). Also included here are such government-inspired organizations as the 31st December Women's Movement, an organization created by the wife of Ghana's current president to mobilize women for a variety of development activities.

- *Modern business and professional associations* representing different businesses and professional groupings (e.g., the Bar Association or the Ghana Association of Industries).

Since independence, Ghana's nonprofit sector has experienced radically different political environments, ranging from pro-socialist to pro-market policies. During the 1970s and 1980s, however, the nonprofit sector was subject to many government restrictions. Specifically, Law 221, issued by the military government, forbade the establishment and operation of private voluntary associations, including churches, unless specifically authorized by a government-appointed commission. While Law 221 was applied less strictly beginning in the late 1980s, it was not until the early 1990s that the nonprofit sector could operate more or less without direct government interference. As part of an ambitious economic restructuring program that is sponsored by the World Bank and other donor agencies, the government is now increasingly calling on nonprofit organizations to assist in the implementation of agricultural and community development projects. Supported by an influx of international funds, both public and private, this has led to a considerable redesign of the relationship between the government and the nonprofit sector: from adversaries to cautious partners.

Few systematic data are available on Ghana's nonprofit sector. To be sure, it includes numerous, typically unregistered indigenous organizations which exist in every village and urban neighbor-hood. In addition, there are 114 nonprofit hospitals scattered throughout the country, and 242 primary and 229 secondary schools, largely connected with Christian churches. Beyond this, the Ghana Association for Private Voluntary Organizations in Development claims over 100 NGO organizations alone.

India

Few countries have a nonprofit sector with the cultural and historical richness of India's. Voluntarism has deep roots in Hindu culture, reaching back to the early Hindu empires of Maurya and Gupta. Until the colonial period, education, health, culture, and relief efforts remained largely the domain of voluntary and charitable institutions affiliated with family, caste, trade guilds, and religion. In addition to Hinduism, Islam, Christianity, and other religions have made their institutional mark on India's nonprofit sector.[14] These different religious and cultural currents are reflected in a nonprofit sector that includes:

- *Caste associations*, which, particularly after independence, became mobilizing points for the disadvantaged and untouchables in Indian society, promoting their social and political standing;
- A large network of *Gandhian organizations*, which advocate voluntary action as a way to promote rural development by constructing self-supporting and self-governing village communities;
- Church-related, *Christian nonprofit organizations*, which entered the country under colonial patronage, and which continue to maintain a presence in the country's educational and health care system;
- A set of *separatist and religiously based nonprofit organizations* among the country's Hindu and Islamic populations, which are advancing claims for separate educational and social service systems;
- Large *humanitarian relief agencies* that emerged in the 1960s, due to a sequence of famines, floods and other disasters that struck India at that time, and the influx of large numbers of refugees from neighboring countries;
- *"Empowerment-oriented,"* often politicized, nonprofit organizations, which originated in the 1970s, when the nonprofit form

became a popular way to organize the various social and political movements present in the country at that time;
- *Development-oriented NGOs*; and
- *Professional associations* of many different sorts.

In contrast to many other developing countries, the Indian state, with the exception of a brief period under Indira Gandhi, has left substantial room for the formation of civil society organizations. Given the tremendous religious, ethnic, and political complexity of Indian society, and the continued economic strains imposed on large parts of the population, both government and the various components of the nonprofit sector find themselves in a delicate relationship. Fearful of outside interference and the use of nonprofit organizations, especially NGOs, for political ends, the government has sought ways to "macro-manage" the country's nonprofit sector and "depoliticize" it by restricting the role of political organizations. The Foreign Contributions Regulation Act of 1976 (amended in 1985) was meant to do just that by monitoring the inflow of foreign funds to Indian organizations. The act allows the government to ban the receipt of funds from abroad for politically suspect nonprofit organizations.

At the same time, the government, particularly the Congress Party, has encouraged the role of nonprofit organizations, particularly in development, by providing greater direct financial support. However, to make sure that the nonprofit presence in development activities does not restrict the growth of the for-profit sector, the government removed all tax exemptions from income-generating activities by nonprofit organizations, which has restricted their access to income and potentially limited their role in promoting economic development.

Despite these limitations, the scope of the Indian nonprofit sector is vast. One handbook lists nearly 1,000 environmental organizations alone. Another identifies over 2,200 Gandhian organizations. The World Bank alone works directly with over 400 organizations. For the country as a whole, the number of nonprofit organizations must be well over 1,000,000.

Thailand

Whereas in the past, Thailand's various military regimes often viewed the nonprofit sector with mistrust, it is now increasingly recognized as a key component to the country's social and economic development. Several types of nonprofit organizations exist in Thailand:[15]

- *Associations*, which must declare their nonpolitical character upon registration and include a wide variety of social, cultural, and recreational purposes. As of 1989, the number of associations was about 8,500.

- *Foundations*, which are traditionally established in honor of distinguished Thai citizens and provide welfare and relief to the population; promote education, culture, and, more recently, environmental protection; and foster economic development. In 1989, close to 3,000 (2,966) foundations were registered in Thailand.

- *Business and labor organizations*, which include industry promotion councils, employers associations, and unions.

- *Cremation societies*, which are deeply rooted in Buddhist traditions and prescribe detailed ceremonies for the proper care of deceased bodies. Joining one of the 2,773 cremation societies is a popular way to assure that one's religious rites are performed correctly. But these societies also perform wider social service functions and sometimes take on other functions as well, such as providing financial services and agricultural extension in rural areas.

- *Unregistered associations*, which are known as working groups, units, or forums. These include grass-roots organizations and advocacy groups concerned with human rights and local development, as well as Buddhist institutions such as village temples or monasteries (*wat*).

The Thai nonprofit sector has grown significantly in recent decades, and its expansion has increased over the last few years. In fact, 86 percent of all foundations, 74 percent of registered associations, and 84 percent of all nonregistered associations have been established since 1973. Indeed, associations seem to be growing at the rate of 7 percent per year and foundations at the rate of 10 percent—faster than the country's economy. Though long treated with suspicion by the state, nonprofit organizations have increasingly come to be seen as useful vehicles not only to promote development, but increasingly to help relieve the social and economic difficulties that development can also produce.

Conclusion

Quite clearly, it is impossible in the limited compass available here to convey the rich complexity of the nonprofit sector as it has evolved in the 12 societies that have been the focus of our initial work. Perhaps, however, this brief "sampler" of some of the salient features of this sector in the different countries will at least sensitize readers to the very different dynamics underlying the broad patterns outlined in the previous chapters. In doing so, however, it should also convey the central conclusion that, whatever its particular origins or national characteristics, what we have here termed the nonprofit sector seems everywhere to be experiencing a significant upward growth.

Notes

1 Lester M. Salamon, "The Rise of the Nonprofit Sector," *Foreign Affairs*, Vol. 73, No. 44 (July/August, 1994), pp. 2–16.

2 For a fuller discussion of the French nonprofit sector, see Edith Archambault, "Defining the Nonprofit Sector: France," in Lester M. Salamon and Helmut K. Anheier, eds., *Working Papers of the Johns Hopkins Comparative Nonprofit Sector Project*, No. 7 (Baltimore: The Johns Hopkins Institute for Policy Studies, 1993).

3 Edith Archambault, "First Results: Giving and Volunteering Survey," I.S.L.—Fondation de France—L.E.S. (Paris, Laboratoire Economie Sociale, Université de Paris, 1991), mimeographed.

4 For further analysis of the German nonprofit sector, see Helmut K. Anheier and Wolfgang Seibel, "Defining the Nonprofit Sector: Germany," in Lester M. Salamon and Helmut K. Anheier, eds., *Working Papers of the Johns Hopkins Comparative Nonprofit Sector Project*, No. 6 (Baltimore: The Johns Hopkins Institute for Policy Studies, 1993). For a discussion of the "marketization of welfare," see Lester M. Salamon, "The Marketization of Welfare: Changing Nonprofit and For-Profit Roles in the American Welfare State," *Social Service Review*, Vol. 67, No. 1 (March 1993), pp. 17–39.

5 For a fuller discussion of the Italian nonprofit sector, see Gian Paolo Barbetta, "Defining the Nonprofit Sector: Italy," in Lester M. Salamon and Helmut K. Anheier, eds., *Working Papers of the Johns Hopkins Comparative Nonprofit Sector Project*, No. 8 (Baltimore: The Johns Hopkins Institute for Policy Studies, 1993).

6 This picture would change significantly if we were to shift into the health subsector a portion of the nursing homes now grouped under "social services," as outlined more fully in note 10, p. 60.

7 Takayoshi Amenomori, "Defining the Nonprofit Sector: Japan," in Lester M. Salamon and Helmut K. Anheier, eds., *Working Papers of the Johns Hopkins Comparative Nonprofit Sector Project*, No. 15 (Baltimore: The Johns Hopkins Institute for Policy Studies, 1993).

8 For a fuller discussion of the U.K. charitable organization structure, see Jeremy Kendall and Martin Knapp, "Defining the Nonprofit Sector: The United Kingdom," in Lester M. Salamon and Helmut K. Anheier, eds., *Working Papers of the Johns Hopkins Comparative Nonprofit Sector Project*, No. 5 (Baltimore: The Johns Hopkins Institute for Policy Studies, 1993).

9 The description provided here is drawn largely from Lester M. Salamon, *America's Nonprofit Sector: A Primer* (New York: The Foundation Center, 1992).

10 For further discussion of the Hungarian nonprofit sector, see Éva Kuti, "Defining the Nonprofit Sector: Hungary," in Lester M. Salamon and Helmut K. Anheier, eds., *Working Papers of the Johns Hopkins Comparative Nonprofit Sector Project*, No. 13 (Baltimore: The Johns Hopkins Institute for Policy Studies, 1993).

11 For further discussion on the Brazilian nonprofit sector, see Leilah Landim, "Defining the Nonprofit Sector: Brazil," in Lester M. Salamon and Helmut K. Anheier, eds., *Working Papers of the Johns Hopkins Comparative Nonprofit Sector Project*, No. 9 (Baltimore: The Johns Hopkins Institute for Policy Studies, 1993).

12 Wanderley Guilherme Santos, "Publico e Privado no Sistema Brasileiro" [Public and Private in the Brazilian System] (Rio de Janeiro, 1990), mimeographed.

13 For further detail on the Egyptian nonprofit sector, see Amani Kandil, "Defining the Nonprofit Sector: Egypt," in Lester M. Salamon and Helmut K. Anheier, eds., *Working Papers of the Johns Hopkins Comparative Nonprofit Sector Project*, No. 10 (Baltimore: The Johns Hopkins Institute for Policy Studies, 1993).

14 For a more detailed discussion on the nonprofit sector in India, see Siddhartha Sen, "Defining the Nonprofit Sector: India," in Lester M. Salamon and Helmut K. Anheier, eds., *Working Papers of the Johns Hopkins Comparative Nonprofit Sector Project*, No. 12 (Baltimore: The Johns Hopkins Institute for Policy Studies, 1993).

15 For a full discussion on nonprofit organizations in Thailand, see Amara Pongsapich, "Defining the Nonprofit Sector: Thailand," in Lester M. Salamon and Helmut K. Anheier, eds., *Working Papers of the Johns Hopkins Comparative Nonprofit Sector Project*, No. 11 (Baltimore: The Johns Hopkins Institute for Policy Studies, 1993).

Chapter 7

ISSUES AND IMPLICATIONS

As the previous chapters of this books have shown, a remarkable upsurge has taken place throughout the world in organized, voluntary activity, in the formation and growth of private nonprofit organizations of many different sorts. The nonprofit sector now constitutes a powerful economic force in settings as diverse as highly centralized France and Japan and highly decentralized Germany and the United States. In the developing world and the former Communist bloc as well, nonprofit organizations are now being recognized as potent mechanisms for stimulating development and fostering civic involvement. Indeed, as one of the present authors has recently put it, "The rise of the nonprofit sector may well prove to be as significant a development of the latter twentieth century as the rise of the nation-state was of the latter nineteenth century."[1]

While the evidence reported here suggests the enormous scale and importance that the nonprofit sector, as we have defined it, has attained in widely disparate settings, it also suggests a number of issues that this sector faces at the present time and in the years immediately ahead. Some of these issues arise from the sector's external environment. Others arise from the sector's own internal operations. Given the heady expectations that have recently been placed on this set of institutions, it is important to identify these issues and spell out some of the implications they hold.

To do so, we draw on dozens of interviews conducted by our field associates of nonprofit leaders, government officials, and other informed people in each of our project countries as well as our own observations about the state of the nonprofit sector in the countries we have examined. As such, this discussion inevitably takes us a step or two beyond the simple factual data that has been the principal focus of prior chapters. In doing so, our intent is not to pronounce the final word on matters that will have to be settled within separate national contexts, but rather to provide an agenda around which a productive debate can begin.

In particular, our research leads us to identify eight crucial issues that confront the nonprofit sector around the world at the present time. While these issues vary greatly in salience and importance from country to country, they are present to some degree almost everywhere and consequently form a core agenda that those concerned about the future of the nonprofit sector might usefully address.

Out of the shadows

At the most fundamental level, the nonprofit sector in much of the world continues to face a significant problem of visibility and public awareness. So dominant has the prevailing two-sector model of social life been in most countries that the existence, let alone the scale and dimensions, of a definable "third sector" of private nonprofit organizations has been largely overlooked. Even in the United States, where the concept of a not-for-profit sector has at least been recognized for some time, basic information on this sector was nonexistent until the early 1980s. Even now the sector is not covered explicitly in national income accounts,[2] and its true character and role are only dimly perceived. In other countries, the level of information available about this sector is even less well developed. The sector is systematically ignored in national economic statistics, rarely mentioned in public debate, and overlooked almost entirely in public education and most scholarly research.

To some degree, this lack of attention serves the sector's interests well, shielding it from unwanted scrutiny and protecting it from the questioning that such scrutiny might provoke. In the long run, however, lack of public awareness cannot but cause the sector problems. This is, after all, preeminently the "citizen's sector." As such, it cannot afford to be incomprehensible and invisible to most citizens, or to those who represent them in the public arena. To the contrary, in order to attract popular support, nonprofit organizations must first attract popular attention and concern.

Fortunately, some evidence of growing awareness of this sector is apparent in the countries we have examined in this project. This is perhaps most strikingly apparent in France, where a strong Jacobin tradition long prejudiced citizens and policymakers against voluntary organization and toward reliance on the state. During the past two decades, and particularly since 1981 when the Socialists came to power, however, successive French governments have systematically sought to rehabilitate the reputation of nonprofit organizations. Thus, encouragement was given in 1970 for the formation of the *Comité national de liaison des activités mutualistes, coopératives et associatives* (CNLAMCA) to represent the "social economy" sector before the public authorities. A 1975 Prime Ministerial circular acknowledged that "the state and the public communities have no monopoly on the public good. In many cases, private initiative came first to meet people's needs."[3] Then, in 1981, the Mitterand government created the *Délégation à l'Economie Sociale*, an interministerial agency to promote the social economy sector. In 1983, this sector was given representation on the *Conseil Economique et Social*, France's "third parliament." At the same time a general fund was created to promote associative life (*Fonds national pour le développement de la vie associative*). While hardly overwhelming in their scale, these actions helped to conceptualize and legitimize the "third sector" in the eyes both of the public and the political elite.

While similar actions have also been evident elsewhere (e.g., the Japanese government's decision to permit tax deductions for corporate charitable contributions beginning in 1989, the Italian government's passage of Law 266 creating a more formal legal status for the numerous *organizzazioni de volontariato*, and the growing acceptance of NGOs as legitimate development partners in Ghana), the fact remains that broad-based understanding of the role and character of nonprofit organizations remains the exception rather than the rule. To correct this, concerted action will be needed. At a minimum, this will require the production, regularly and reliably, of the kind of basic information on the sector's scope, size, structure, and role presented here, preferably using certain common conventions from place to place to allow the kinds of comparisons we have been able to make. Producing such information should ultimately become a responsibility of national statistical offices, as it is already for the two other major sectors, though other arrangements may be necessary until they are ready to take on the task. Beyond this, however, proactive efforts will be needed by the nonprofit sector itself—to improve public awareness of its role and introduce both citizens at large and key public and private leaders to its functions and operations. This will require explicit public information campaigns, in separate national settings, and internationally as well. It will also require conscious efforts to boost support for research on this set of organizations in order to create teaching materials and generally establish the "third sector" as a legitimate focus of scholarly work.

Establishing legitimacy

One reason for the lack of awareness of nonprofit organizations in many countries is the legal limbo in which these organizations are forced to operate. Clear legal appreciation of the nature of these organizations and the rights to which they are entitled are the exceptions rather than the rule around the world. While the chartering of nonprofit organizations is reasonably open in the common law countries, many civil law countries erect significant barriers. Japan is perhaps the clearest example among the countries examined here of a legal structure that impedes rather than encourages the creation of nonprofit institutions. From the perspective of Japanese law, the formation of such organizations is treated not as a right but as a privilege to be granted or denied by governmental authorities based on their view of the value of the organizations to the government. That these organizations might have value to citizens that justifies their existence regardless of official opinion is not a concept that finds much acknowledgment in the Japanese legal tradition. Similar impediments are evident in Egypt's Law 32 and in the requirements for approval of the Ministry of Social Welfare before nonprofit organizations can be registered in Ghana. In Italy, a similar legal ambiguity has kept most associations from incorporating, creating a vast "informal" nonprofit sector outside the reach of both citizens and the state. Even in France, where legal treatment of nonprofit organizations has become far more favorable in recent decades, the formation of foundations continues to be constrained, and most nonprofit organizations are prevented from acquiring endowments to help guarantee a degree of financial security to their operations.

While governments certainly have legitimate bases to require accountability and adherence to clear standards of public service on the part of nonprofit organizations in return for the special tax or other benefits they grant, they should be encouraged to establish regularized and generally supportive procedures for the formation and operation of such organizations. In modern society, the right to associate, to form nonprofit organizations, has come to be a critical prerequisite for democratic governance and a functioning civil society, as basic as the right of free expression and in some sense a necessary corollary of it. Without a predictable and generally open legal environment, nonprofit development is likely to be severely constrained or unduly distorted. Establishing such an environment should therefore be a priority wherever one does not now exist.

Beyond the paradigm of conflict

In addition to improving the legal environment in which nonprofit organizations operate, broader efforts are needed to establish a meaningful collaborative relationship between the nonprofit sector and the state. As a first step in this direction, it will be necessary to clear the conceptual space for such collaboration.

As we have seen, governmental support and encouragement have been crucial to the development of the nonprofit sector almost everywhere, including the United States. Yet, a deep-seated ideological current posits a fundamental conflict between the nonprofit sector and the state and discourages cooperation between the two. This line of argument has been regularly used, particularly by conservative opponents of the welfare state, to justify assaults on government social welfare spending on grounds that it destroys the viability of nonprofit organizations and other "mediating institutions."[4] In practice, however, while a certain tension necessarily exists between these two sectors, the assumption of inevitable conflict and the emphasis on the conflictual elements of the relationship over the potentially collaborative ones can lead to the loss of important social possibilities.

This point has been nicely illustrated by the path of welfare state expansion in the United States in the 1960s and by the recent embrace of the nonprofit sector by the Socialist government of François Mitterand in France. In the face of strong ideological resistance to state welfare, Great Society reformers in the United States in the 1960s built an elaborate system of "third-party government" in which the national government financed a sizable array of welfare services but turned to other institutions, among them private, nonprofit organizations, to deliver the resulting services.[5] In this way, it was possible to expand America's relatively meager social welfare protections without expanding the size of the state bureaucracy. France's left-wing government pursued a similar course in the 1980s. Rather than shying away from the nonprofit sector as an expression of right-wing idealism, French Socialists seized on this sector as a mechanism for permitting the extension of welfare-state services without the need to expand the increasingly mistrusted apparatus of the modern welfare state. Far from being an alternative to the state, the voluntary sector thus came to be seen instead as an ally.

A far different course was pursued, however, by the conservative regimes of Ronald Reagan in the United States and, to a lesser extent, Margaret Thatcher in the U.K. For Reagan, the nonprofit sector became a stalking horse for a broad-gauged assault on state-financed welfare services. Support for the nonprofit sector was thus advanced as an excuse for limiting the role of the state. In the process, the fiscal base of the American nonprofit sector was conveniently misportrayed and the impression created that American nonprofits rely chiefly, or even exclusively, on private charitable support—a position clearly at odds with the facts, as the data presented here have shown. Not only did this mislead unsuspecting outside observers, but it also threatened to discredit the whole concept of voluntarism and nonprofit action by converting them into an ideological cover for conservative policy objectives.

For those concerned about the long-term viability of this sector, the lesson should be clear. While care must be taken to avoid the too-close embrace of the voluntary sector by the state, equal care must be taken to avoid the "cold shoulder" as well.

From agent to partner

Cooperation with the state is not, however, a sufficient posture for the nonprofit sector. This is the message that emerges from the recent history of Japan, where nonprofit organizations have been actively enlisted in the provision of state-financed services, but always on terms defined mostly, indeed almost exclusively, by the state. The upshot is to convert nonprofit organizations into mere "agents" of the state, rather than true "partners" with it. Thus, for example, Japan's social welfare corporations (*shakaifukushi hōjin*) are so restricted to performing tasks assigned to them by central and local governments that they think of themselves more as quasi-governmental organizations than private nonprofit organizations, even though this is their legal form.[6]

Few issues are as crucial to the future of the nonprofit sector, in fact, as this one of determining how to fashion cooperation with the state in a way that protects the nonprofit sector from surrendering its basic autonomy and thus allows it to function as a true partner with the state and not simply as an "agent" or "vendor." This issue has become a vital one in the U.K., where a shift from outright grant aid to purchase-of-service contracting has occasioned complaints that government is undermining the independence of nonprofit providers and threatening the sector's advocacy function. In the U.S. as well, conservative critics regularly fault government support of nonprofit organizations on grounds that it distorts the organizations' basic missions and character. Underlying these concerns is a conviction that nonprofit organizations involved in the delivery of publicly funded services should have meaningful opportunities to shape the structure and content of the services being provided rather than simply be required to follow government-determined recipes. As a recent National Council for Voluntary Organizations publication put it in the U.K.: "In a partnership all partners should be given the opportunity to influence programme aims and objectives."[7]

Three models are fortunately available for moving government-nonprofit relationships from "agency" to "partnership" status in these terms. The first is the German "corporatist" model, in which the six "free welfare associations" have established a formal collaborative body with which the government is obligated to consult in the development of all major social legislation. In this way at least the major networks of nonprofit organizations in the country are guaranteed a ringside seat in the development of the policies they will ultimately implement. A second model is the American "interest group" model. No formal channels exist for nonprofit input into the shaping of public policy in the United States, and no umbrella group representing the whole of the nonprofit sector takes effective part in most policy discussions. Instead, the policy arena is fragmented into a number of "policy subsystems," each of which is now characterized by a relatively high degree of porousness. Nonprofit organizations operating in these various spheres represent interests whose support is often sought, or whose opposition must frequently be accommodated, in the passage of legislation and the maintenance of program budgets. They consequently have significant opportunities to influence legislative outcomes and bring matters to legislative attention, but always in an ad hoc, unstructured fashion in which a great deal is left to the vagaries of timing and effective representation, and to the relative strengths of the various contending parties. Finally, a third model is at least contemplated in the "Scrutiny Report" recently issued by the U.K. Home Office.[8] In a sense, the Scrutiny Commission contemplates a model that is midway between the American and the German. No corporatist consultative body is proposed, but an effort is made to get beyond the purely ad hoc American pattern by requiring that government agencies that fund nonprofit organizations clarify more precisely the goals and objectives being sought through their programs and the expectations of the nonprofit organizations working with them. In return, nonprofit organizations agree to adhere to these objectives in the operation of the programs. At the same time, the Scrutiny Report proposes to continue two additional features of the U.K. system that are not present in the American model—an official body in the Home Office (the Voluntary Services Unit) specifically charged with coordinating government policies toward the voluntary sector; and governmental support for a set of "infrastructure institutions" that help promote the nonprofit sector and equip it to respond to governmental initiatives both at the national and local levels. This includes the National Council for Voluntary Organizations and local councils for voluntary service.

Each of these models has, of course, its advantages and

disadvantages. The German model guarantees substantial government consultation with key components of the nonprofit sector, but the consultation is restricted to the more established components of the sector and leads to a highly conservative posture toward existing program structures. The U.S. model is far more open and free-wheeling, but fails to develop any coherence either in government's treatment of the nonprofit sector or in the nonprofit sector's relations with government. Indeed, it produces a highly piecemeal approach to major social ills. The U.K. model offers an attractive compromise with a bit of the policy coherence and consultation of the German model and a bit of the openness of the American one, but this compromise has yet to be put into effective operation.

Which of these "models" is best depends, of course, on particular local circumstances. The central point, however, is that nonprofit organizations must not be content simply with a role as "agent" of the state. To the extent such a posture comes to define their role, they will lose much of their special raison d'être. What is needed instead is the elaboration of a more collaborative mode of operation. But this will require continued pursuit of an active policy role on the part of nonprofit organizations and a willingness to accommodate nonprofit inputs into the framing of policy on the part of the state.

Buttressing the philanthropic base

Perhaps the most effective way to ensure a reasonable partnership between the voluntary sector and the state is for the voluntary sector to develop its own alternative sources of support. One of these alternatives is earned income from fees or sale of products. The other is private charitable support, whether from individuals, corporations, or foundations.

So far as the former is concerned, the data presented in this report make clear that the nonprofit sector has already moved rather far down this road. Private fees are the single most important source of nonprofit income at the international level. For five of the seven countries examined in depth here, private fee income outdistances all other sources of support, and for the remaining two it is a close second. For most of the countries, such earned income takes the form of fees for core services that the nonprofit organizations provide—e.g., tuition for university education, fees for day care, payments for hospital treatment. In Hungary, where the ability of service recipients to pay is very limited and alternative sources of support unavailable, earned income takes the form of proceeds from business enterprises that nonprofit organizations operate.

Where nonprofits are providing services to populations that can afford to pay, fees and service charges make a great deal of sense. At the same time, excessive reliance on this form of income can lead nonprofit organizations too far from their "charitable" roots and diminish their ability to respond to the needs of the disadvantaged. Similarly, the use of "unrelated" business income as the principal source of nonprofit support can drain precious management talent away from the organization's principal mission and open the sector to charges of unfair competition with private businesses. Such charges have become a significant political issue in the United States, and the use of the foundation form to shield businesses from taxation in Hungary has recently led to a serious backlash against the entire nonprofit field.

What all of this suggests is the need to ensure a vigorous base of private philanthropic support in order to guarantee a reasonable degree of independence and autonomy for the nonprofit sector. To be sure, private giving often comes with its own "strings" attached. However, balanced against government and earned income, it can help provide a zone of autonomy that is crucial for the health of the sector. The exact level of private funding required for this purpose is, of course, difficult to specify. Clearly, it is unreasonable to expect that private giving will constitute all, or even most, nonprofit income. Even in the United States, the country credited with having the most supportive laws and traditions for private giving, such support constitutes only 19 percent of overall nonprofit revenue. At the same time, a level much below 10 percent is probably insufficient to provide the financial "cushion" that a healthy and vital nonprofit sector probably requires.

As it turns out, however, only three of the seven countries we examined in depth—the U.S., the U.K., and Hungary—had levels of private giving that exceeded this "minimum" range, and the Hungarian case is probably an artifact of the smallness of the

nonprofit sector rather than a sign of vigorous private philanthropic activity. Significantly, moreover, the countries with the
lowest levels of private giving also have the least generous tax
incentives for such giving. Thus, in Japan, where private giving
constitutes a minuscule 1 percent of nonprofit income, contributions to nonprofit organizations are deductible from taxes only
for corporations, and even then only up to certain limits. For
individuals, contributions are deductible only for a very narrow
range of organizations, the so-called *tokutei kōeki zōshin hōjin*, or
special public-interest-promoting organizations, and these are
quite few. Similarly, in Italy tax deductibility is limited to only
certain classes of nonprofit organizations (e.g., those active in the
performing arts or in the preservation of prominent art works)
and even then only up to 2 percent of personal income.[9] French
law is somewhat more lenient. However, declared associations
are forbidden from owning real estate or receiving legacies, and
charitable contributions to them are deductible only up to 3
percent of taxable income. Although a special class of "public
utility associations" exists with the ability to own real estate and
other financial assets, access to this classification requires the
approval of the *Conseil d'Etat* and a two-year application procedure. The result is to deny nonprofit organizations the kind of
long-term support that endowments can provide, limiting severely the growth of charitable foundations.

While liberalization of tax incentives will hardly guarantee an
upsurge of private charitable contributions, a reasonable case
can be made that such liberalization makes sound policy sense if
the nonprofit sector is to become a truly viable social and economic force with the ability to retain a meaningful degree of
independence while cooperating with government in the pursuit
of joint objectives. At the same time, other steps will be needed
as well in order to change public attitudes and foster a greater
sense of responsibility for the support of nonprofit institutions.
This can take the form of educational programs in the schools
and use of the mass media. Campaigns of the sort launched by
Minister of Social Economy Bernard Kouchner in France to con-
vince schoolchildren to bring rice for the poor in Africa also have
their place. Stimulating awareness of the importance of giving
and volunteering could usefully be one of the major functions of
charitable foundations and umbrella groups representing the

sector. Without such efforts, the danger is great that the ethos of giving will fail to develop regardless of changes in tax and other laws.

Ensuring accountability

Whatever the tax laws or exhortations to contribute, the ability of nonprofit organizations to attract charitable contributions or retain governmental support will depend heavily on the sensitivity they show to the need for public confidence in their activities. At a minimum, this will require greater "transparency" on the part of both foundations and associations. One of the historic complaints about the nonprofit sector has been the secrecy that surrounds its activities, the sense that these organizations abuse the public benefits they receive for essentially private purposes. Recent scandals involving the payment of excessive salaries and benefits to nonprofit officials in the United States, mismanagement of blood supplies in France, misuse of the foundation form to shield business activities from taxation in Hungary, and excessive intimacy between nonprofit organizations and political party patrons in Italy have unfortunately played into these complaints and put a cloud over this set of institutions. More generally, significant components of the nonprofit sector continue to operate with the mentality of a "private preserve" rather than a set of publicly responsible institutions enjoying significant public benefits. Thus, for example, the first full directory of German foundations was published only in 1992, and many foundations chose not to disclose even very basic programmatic and financial information. What is more, the introduction to this document includes a passage intended to discourage readers from using the compiled information for grantseeking activities, conveying the impression that knowledge about the resources available from foundations was somehow privileged information.[10] Similarly, a recent effort by the Commission of the European Union to compile basic information on nonprofit organizations in the member countries encountered serious resistance in both Italy and Germany. Such secrecy simply fuels distrust toward the nonprofit sector and limits the prospects for its further development.

While foundations and other nonprofit organizations have

legitimate rights to a degree of privacy and freedom from state scrutiny, they also have an obligation to be forthcoming about their basic finances and operations, and to operate in accord with high ethical standards. Without this, every manner of suspicion and rumor will be fair game, with results that can be quite harmful to the sector, as recent developments in Hungary, in the United States, and in the European Parliament clearly demonstrate.[11] Ideally, such openness and ethical behavior can be arrived at voluntarily, through codes of conduct formulated by the sector and enforced by its own institutions. Lacking this, however, minimum public reporting requirements are probably appropriate.

Professionalization

Closely related to the issue of "transparency" is the issue of "professionalization" within the nonprofit sector. Although employees in nonprofit organizations in such countries as Germany and Japan essentially function like civil servants and receive comparable training and compensation, in most other countries employment in the nonprofit sector is often characterized by low salaries, limited benefits, and nonexistent training. This is certainly the case in France, where the small scale of most nonprofit organizations, the weakness of trade unionism within the sector, the fact that most employees are women, and the commitment employees have to the objectives of the organization translate into lower pay scales and more restricted benefits. What is more, explicit staff training has traditionally been quite limited within this sector. Indeed, these features have been defended as part of the special appeal of nonprofit organizations— —their reliance on volunteers and resulting informal character, their avoidance of rigid professional norms, and their consequent flexibility.

While these arguments are appealing, however, they are also short-sighted. As nonprofit organizations move more into the center of societal problem-solving, the pressures on them to become more effective and more "professional" will increase. What is more, managers of nonprofit organizations will need to understand not simply the general rudiments of good management, but also the special features of nonprofit management—the distinctive history and rationale for this kind of organization and the special requirements they have in such areas as fundraising, advocacy, dealing with volunteers, and dealing with boards of directors.

To cope with this need, specialized training programs for nonprofit managers have emerged in the United States, the United Kingdom, and other countries. But the training and information challenges facing this sector have only begun to be addressed. Far more energetic efforts will also be needed to expand the training opportunities available, to institutionalize the training function within the sector and within individual organizations, and to sensitize personnel to the special tasks that this form of management entails. What seems certain is that, over the long run, few activities will pay greater returns.

Globalization

Finally, in an increasingly interdependent world, the nonprofit sector, no less than the for-profit one, faces immense global challenges. While nonprofit organizations typically focus on domestic issues, these issues are increasingly affected by cross-border considerations. This is true, for example, of environmental pollution, migration of foreign workers, and the impact of changing terms of trade on the viability of local rural development projects. Beyond this, as corporate enterprises become multinational, the ability of nonprofit organizations to capture corporate charitable contributions will depend on their ability to meet standards set in distant nations. The same is true of grants and contracts from multinational bodies such as the World Bank and the United Nations Development Program or from supranational entities like the Social Fund of the European Union. Under these circumstances, the pressures have increased to establish a degree of uniformity in the legal provisions affecting nonprofit organizations from place to place.

Nonprofit organizations operating in the international development field have long since formulated procedures for dealing with these cross-national programming and funding challenges. Their experience will be crucial for other organizations seeking to operate across national borders as well. Beyond this, the European Union has proposed a European Association Statute that would create a class of transnational "European associations," able to operate at the European level. More troubling to many is a similar proposal (the so-called Coimbra report) that would require foundations in Europe to secure the status of "European Utility" from the European Parliament or Commission and that would set up a "European Centre" to "harmonize foundations carrying out similar activities."[12]

Whether these or other provisions make sense, the fact remains that nonprofit organizations cannot afford to ignore the global developments taking place around them. In one fashion or another, they must adjust their operations to cope with an increasingly interconnected global scene.

Conclusion

Fundamental historical forces—a widespread loss of confidence in the state, expanding communications, the emergence of a more vibrant commercial and professional middle class, and increased demands for a wide range of specialized services—have come together in recent years to expand the role of private, nonprofit organizations in virtually every part of the world. Such organizations enjoy distinctive advantages in delivering human services, responding to citizen pressures, and giving expression to citizen demands. As a consequence, the nonprofit sector has come into its own as a major social and economic force, with substantial and growing employment and a significant share of the responsibility for responding to public needs.

While this set of organizations has grown in both scope and scale, however, it still faces immense challenges—challenges that are both conceptual and practical, immediate and long-term. In many places, the very concept of this sector remains ill-defined and the legal structures for accommodating it unformed. Elsewhere the sector has become a pivotal mechanism for delivering massive quantities of government-funded human services yet still lacks even the basic rudiments for autonomous, independent action.

Whatever the particular circumstance, however, it seems clear that the demands being placed on this set of institutions is expanding far faster than the sector's ability to respond. Under these circumstances, a clear understanding of what this sector is, and what its capabilities are, becomes a necessary first step to the broader processes of change that are needed. Contributing to this first step has been the objective of this report and the project on which it is based. Our hope is that this will at least provide part of the foundation on which others can now build.

Notes

1 Lester M. Salamon, "The Rise of the Nonprofit Sector," *Foreign Affairs*, Vol. 74, No. 3 (Summer 1994), p. 111.

2 Helen Stone Tice, "The Nonprofit Sector in a National Accounts Framework," *Voluntas*, Vol. 4, No. 4 (1993), pp. 445–464.

3 Quoted in Marie-Thérèse Cheroutre, "Exercice et développement de la vie associative dans le cadre de la loi du ler/07/1901" (Paris: Conseil Economique et Social, 24/02/1993).

4 This line of argument is developed in Robert Nisbet, *Community and Power*, 2d edition (New York: Oxford University Press, 1962). For a critique of this line of argument, see Lester M. Salamon, "Of Market Failure, Government Failure, and Third-Party Government: Toward a Theory of Government-Nonprofit Relations in the Modern Welfare State," *Journal of Voluntary Action Research*, Vol. 16, Nos. 1 and 2 (January 1987), pp. 29–49, reprinted in Lester M. Salamon, *Partners in Public Service* (Baltimore: The Johns Hopkins University Press, 1995).

5 For a more detailed examination of this pattern, see Lester M. Salamon, "Rethinking Public Management: Third-Party Government and the Changing Forms of Public Action," *Public Policy*, Vol. 29, No. 3 (1981), pp. 255–275; Lester M. Salamon, *Beyond Privatization: The Tools of Government Action* (Washington, D.C.: The Urban Institute Press, 1989).

6 Takayoshi Amenomori, "Defining the Nonprofit Sector: Japan," in Lester M. Salamon and Helmut K. Anheier eds., *Working Papers of the Johns Hopkins Comparative Nonprofit Sector Project*, No. 15 (Baltimore: The Johns Hopkins Institute for Policy Studies, 1993), p. 9.

7 John Mabbott, *Improving Government Funding: Report and Recommendations* (London: National Council for Voluntary Organisations, 1992).

8 H.M. Home Office, *Profiting from Partnership: Efficiency Scrutiny of Government Funding of the Voluntary Sector*, prepared by Juliet Reisz, Richard Boyce, Peter Collings, and Ross Hutchison (London: Her Majesty's Stationery Office, 1990).

9 Gian Paolo Barbetta, "Defining the Nonprofit Sector: Italy," in Lester M. Salamon and Helmut K. Anheier, eds., *Working Papers of the Johns Hopkins Comparative Nonprofit Sector Project*, No. 8 (Baltimore: The Johns Hopkins Institute for Policy Studies, 1993), p. 9.

10 See *Bundesverband Deutscher Stiftungen*, Verzeichnis der Deutschen Stiftungen (Stuttgart: Hoppenstedt Verlag, 1991), p. xviii.

11 In Hungary, liberal laws on foundation tax exemptions have been seriously challenged in the Parliament. In the U.S., claims about unfair competition by nonprofits have led to restrictions on the tax exemption of some nonprofit organizations. In the European Parliament, the recent Coimbra report proposes to restrict significantly the autonomy of foundations in Europe.

12 European Parliament, "Report of the Committee on Culture, Youth, Education and the Media on Foundations and Europe," DOC EN\RR\241\241238 (December 8, 1993), pp. 4–5.

Appendix A
Selected social and economic indicators of project countries

Dimension	France	(West) Germany	Developed market economies			Japan
			Italy	United Kingdom	United States	
Population (million)	56	61	57	57	250	123
% of 20–24 age group enrolled in tertiary education	37.2	33.7	28.6	23.5	63.1	37
% economically active	43.9	49.6	42	49.4	49.9	51.7
GDP ($ billion)	1,191	1,488	1,091	975	5,392	2,943
Per capita income ($)	15,200	16,290	14,550	14,960	21,360	16,950
Total employment (in 1000)	22,931	29,334	21,454	26,881	117,731	62,490
% female employment	40.2	40.1	34.6	43.7	45.4	38.9
Employment by sector % primary sector (agriculture)	6.1	3.4	9.0	2.1	2.8	7.2
% secondary sector (manufacturing)	29.9	39.8	32.4	29.0	26.2	34.1
% tertiary sector (services, trade, government)	64.0	56.8	58.6	68.9	70.9	58.7

Public social expenditure as % of GDP	28.6	23.4	23.3	20.4	12.5	12.2
Political system / Administrative structure / Legal system	unitary centralized civil law	federation decentralized civil law	unitary centralized civil law	unitary centralized common law	federation decentralized common law	unitary centralized civil law
Religious heterogeneity % of population in largest religion	90 (Catholicism)	45 (Catholicism)	99 (Catholicism)	51 (Protestantism)	61 (Protestantism)	96 (Shintoism)
% of population in 2nd largest religion	2	37	–	9.2	25	1
Linguistic heterogeneity % of population in largest language group	100	100	100	100	100	100
number of major languages	1	1	1	1	2	1
Ethnic heterogeneity % of population in largest group	99	99	95	81	85	99
% of population in 2nd largest group	1	1	2	10	12	1

	Post-socialist economy	Developing economies				
Dimension	**Hungary**	**Brazil**	**Ghana**	**Egypt**	**India**	**Thailand**
Population (million)	11	151	14	54	817	55
% of 20–24 age group enrolled in tertiary education	14.7	11.2	1.5	19.6	6.4	16.1
% economically active	45.1	43.2	n/a	27.7	34	55.7
GDP ($ billion)	33	414	6	33	255	80
Per capita income ($)	6,190	4,780	1,720	3,100	1,150	4,610
Total employment (in 1000)	4,978	58,729	307	11,819	259,860	26,297
% female employment	48.4	34.9	n/a	17.6	13.6	43.4
Employment by sector						
% primary sector (agriculture)	18.8	31.0	54.7	34.0	67.0	62.0
% secondary sector (manufacturing)	30.9	27.0	18.7	56	n/a	13.0
% tertiary sector (services, trade, government)	50.3	42.0	26.6	n/a	n/a	25.0
Public social expenditure as % of GDP	16.2	5	n/a	2.6	1.5	0.1

Appendix A

Political system Administrative structure Legal system	unitary centralized civil law	federation decentralized civil law	unitary centralized common law	unitary centralized civil law	federation decentralized common law	unitary centralized civil law
Religious heterogeneity						
% of population in largest religion	68 (Catholicism)	90 (Catholicism)	38 (African Religion)	94 (Islam)	83 (Hindu)	95 (Buddhism)
% of population in 2nd largest religion	25	n/a	30	6	11	4
Linguistic heterogeneity						
% of population in largest language group	98	100	44	100	30	100
number of major languages	1	1	5	2	16	2
Ethnic heterogeneity						
% of population in largest group	97	55	44	90	72	75
% of population in 2nd largest group	2	38	16	10	25	14

Sources:
Population: World Bank, *World Bank Development Report*, 1992; United Nations, *Demographic Yearbook*, 1992
Economy: OECD, *National Accounts, 1980–1992*, 1994; World Bank, *World Bank Development Report*, 1992
Education: UNESCO, *Statistical Yearbook*, 1991
Public Social Spending: ILO, *The Cost of Social Security*, 1993; Eurostat, *Social Protection Expenditures and Receipts*, 1991
Employment: ILO, *Year Book of Labour Statistics*, 1992; CIA, *World Factbook*, 1991; OECD *Economic Survey*, Individual Country Monographs, 1991

Appendix B
The International Classification of
Nonprofit Organizations (ICNPO)

GROUP 1: CULTURE AND RECREATION

1 100 Culture and arts
- media and communications
- visual arts, architecture, ceramic arts
- performing arts
- historical, literary and humanistic societies
- museums
- zoos and aquariums
- multipurpose culture and arts organizations
- support and service organizations, auxiliaries, councils, standard setting and governance organizations
- culture and arts organizations not elsewhere classified

1 200 Recreation
- sports clubs
- recreation/pleasure or social clubs
- multipurpose recreational organizations
- support and service organizations, auxiliaries, councils, standard setting and governance organizations
- recreational organizations not elsewhere classified

1 300 Service clubs
- service clubs
- multipurpose service clubs
- support and service organizations, auxiliaries, councils, standard setting and governance organizations
- service clubs not elsewhere classified

GROUP 2: EDUCATION AND RESEARCH

2 100 Primary and secondary education
- elementary, primary & secondary education

2 200 Higher education
- higher education (university level)

2 300 Other education
- vocational/technical schools

- adult / continuing education
- multipurpose educational organizations
- support and service organizations, auxiliaries, councils, standard setting and governance organizations
- education organizations not elsewhere classified

2 400 Research
- medical research
- science and technology
- social sciences, policy studies
- multipurpose research organizations
- support and service organizations, auxiliaries, councils, standard setting and governance organizations
- research organizations not elsewhere classified

GROUP 3: HEALTH

3 100 Hospitals and rehabilitation
- hospitals
- rehabilitation hospitals

3 200 Nursing homes
- nursing homes

3 300 Mental health and crisis intervention
- psychiatric hospitals
- mental health treatment
- crisis intervention
- multipurpose mental health organizations
- support and service organizations, auxiliaries, councils, standard setting and governance organizations

- mental health organizations not elsewhere classified

3 400 Other health services
- public health and wellness education
- health treatment, primarily outpatient
- rehabilitative medical services
- emergency medical services
- multipurpose health service organizations
- support and service organizations, auxiliaries, councils, standard setting and governance organizations
- health service organizations not elsewhere classified

GROUP 4: SOCIAL SERVICES

4 100 Social services
- child welfare, child services, day care
- youth services and youth welfare
- family services
- services for the handicapped
- services for the elderly
- self-help and other personal social services
- multipurpose social service organizations
- support and service organizations, auxiliaries, councils, standard setting and governance organizations
- social service organizations not elsewhere classified

4 200 Emergency and refugees
- disaster / emergency prevention, relief and control

- temporary shelters
- refugee assistance
- multipurpose emergency and refugee assistance organizations
- support and service organizations, auxiliaries, councils, standard setting and governance organizations
- emergency and refugee assistance organizations not elsewhere classified

4 300 Income support and maintenance

- income support and maintenance
- material assistance
- multipurpose income support and maintenance organizations
- support and service organizations, auxiliaries, councils, standard setting and governance organizations
- income support and maintenance organizations not elsewhere classified

GROUP 5: ENVIRONMENT

5 100 Environment

- pollution abatement and control
- natural resources conservation and protection
- environmental beautification and open spaces
- multipurpose environmental organizations
- support and service organizations, auxiliaries, councils, standard setting and governance organizations
- environmental organizations not elsewhere classified

5 200 Animals

- animal protection and welfare
- wildlife preservation and protection
- veterinary services
- multipurpose animal services organizations
- support and service organizations, auxiliaries, councils, standard setting and governance organizations
- animal-related organizations not elsewhere classified

GROUP 6: DEVELOPMENT AND HOUSING

6 100 Economic, social and community development

- community and neighborhood organizations
- economic development
- social development
- multipurpose economic, social and community development organizations
- support and service organizations, auxiliaries, councils, standard setting and governance organizations
- economic, social and community development organizations not elsewhere classified

6 200 Housing

- housing association
- housing assistance
- multipurpose housing organizations
- support and service organizations, auxiliaries, councils, standard setting and governance organizations

138

- housing organizations not else-where classified

6 300 Employment and training
- job training programs
- vocational counseling and guidance
- vocational rehabilitation and sheltered workshops
- multipurpose employment and training organizations
- support and service organizations, auxiliaries, councils, standard setting and governance organizations
- employment and training organizations not elsewhere classified

GROUP 7: LAW, ADVOCACY AND POLITICS

7 100 Civic and advocacy organizations
- civic associations
- advocacy organizations
- civil rights associations
- ethnic associations
- multipurpose civil and advocacy organizations
- support and service organizations, auxiliaries, councils, standard setting and governance organizations
- civic and advocacy organizations not elsewhere classified

7 200 Law and legal services
- legal services
- crime prevention and public safety
- rehabilitation of offenders
- victim support

- consumer protection associations
- multipurpose law and legal service organizations
- support and service organizations, auxiliaries, councils, standard setting and governance organizations
- law and legal organizations not elsewhere classified

7 300 Political organizations
- political parties
- political action committees
- multipurpose political organizations
- support and service organizations, auxiliaries, councils, standard setting and governance organizations
- political organizations not elsewhere classified

GROUP 8: PHILANTHROPIC INTERMEDIARIES & VOLUNTARISM PROMOTION

8 100 Philanthropic intermediaries
- grantmaking foundations
- voluntarism promotion and support
- fund-raising intermediaries
- multipurpose philanthropic intermediaries and voluntarism organizations
- support and service organizations, auxiliaries, councils, standard setting and governance organizations
- philanthropic intermediary organizations not elsewhere classified

GROUP 9: INTERNATIONAL ACTIVITIES

9 100 International activities
- exchange/friendship/cultural programs
- development assistance associations
- international disaster and relief organizations
- international human rights and peace organizations
- multipurpose international organizations
- support and service organizations, auxiliaries, councils, standard setting and governance organizations
- international organizations not elsewhere classified

GROUP 10: RELIGION

10 100 Religious congregations and associations
- Protestant churches
- Catholic churches
- Jewish synagogues
- Hindu temples
- Shinto shrines
- Arab mosques
- multipurpose religious organizations

- associations of congregations
- support and service organizations, auxiliaries, councils, standard setting and government organizations
- religious organizations not elsewhere classified

GROUP 11: BUSINESS AND PROFESSIONAL ASSOCIATIONS, UNIONS

11 100 Business and professional associations, unions
- business associations
- professional associations
- labor unions
- multipurpose business, professional associations and unions
- support and service organizations, auxiliaries, councils, standard setting and governance organizations
- business, professional associations and unions organizations not elsewhere classified

GROUP 12: [NOT ELSEWHERE CLASSIFIED]

12 100 N.E.C.

Appendix C
Data assembly methodologies

Overview

Our efforts to measure the size, scope and financial base of the nonprofit sector in a broad cross-section of countries included four major conceptual and empirical components:

1. The development of a more inclusive definition of the nonprofit sector than that embodied in the United Nations and European System of National Accounts (see Salamon and Anheier, 1992). According to the structural-operational definition developed for this project, the nonprofit sector is a collection of organizations that are formal, private, nonprofit-distributing, self-governing and voluntary. While this definition would normally include religious congregations and political parties, they were excluded for project purposes.

2. The formulation of a classification system in terms of which nonprofit organizations could be sorted for descriptive and analytical purposes. The need for a classification system was all the more pressing because of the diversity of the nonprofit sector, a diversity that is not captured in existing international systems for classifying economic activity. At the same time, in order to increase the possibility of integrating the nonprofit sector into general economic reporting, we sought to develop a system that was consistent with the existing U.N. International System of Industrial Classifications (ISIC). The resulting classification system, the International Classification of Nonprofit Organizations, or ICNPO, is displayed in Appendix B.

Appendix C

3. The clarification of the various revenue sources of nonprofit organizations. Since the precise meanings and definitions of revenue sources may vary considerably across countries, we tried to follow established OECD and U.N. conventions wherever possible (United Nations, 1993). This applies particularly to the distinction between public and private revenue flows. In particular, following U.N.-OECD conventions (United Nations, 1993, pp. 100–101; 429), we defined government, or the public sector, broadly to refer to all levels and branches of general, regional and local government, including public agencies and corporations, social security funds, national health insurance, and similar public institutions.

In measuring the various revenue sources, we focused primarily on cash or near-cash revenue. Specifically, we differentiated among three major types of sources:

Public sector payments, which include *grants and contracts* (i.e., direct contributions by government to nonprofit organizations in support of specific activities and programs), *statutory transfers* (i.e., contributions by government, as mandated by law, to support nonprofit organizations in carrying out public programs or meeting entitlements), and *third-party payments* (i.e., largely social security and health insurance payments which reimburse an organization for services rendered to individuals).

Private giving, which includes all contributions received from private foundations, businesses, and individuals, either directly or indirectly through federated fund-raising campaigns.

Private fees and payments, which include payments clients make for services they receive that are not compensated by public sector institutions, income from sales of products, dues and similar charges and assessments levied on members of an organization as a condition of membership, as well as investment earnings on assets or endowments owned by an organization.

4. The development and testing of a data assembly strategy to build up estimates of the size of the nonprofit sector so defined and classified. The basic premise of the data assembly strategy was to rely for the most part on already existing data sources and to elaborate on them to yield an empirical picture of the size, scope, and financing of the nonprofit sector. Specifically, this strategy involved three principal features:

- the use of existing employment surveys as the basic building block for the analysis;
- the use of a modular approach to transform the data from these labor surveys into estimates of the expenditure of the nonprofit sector in each of the major fields identified in the ICNPO;
- the separate development of estimates of the revenue base of the sector once the expenditure estimates were developed.

Obviously, the extent to which we could actually implement this general data assembly strategy differed somewhat from country to country, and from field to field, and depended largely on the type and coverage of baseline surveys. Consequently, the exact methodological steps taken to collect data on the size, scope and financial structure of the nonprofit sector and its component parts varied somewhat across research sites and fields. Therefore, the following description of the data assembly strategy for each country is only intended to offer readers a general sense of the data and methodologies involved. A full documentation of data sources, estimation procedures, and other methodological issues will be part of the country monographs and the comparative overview volume to be published by Manchester University Press.

France

In France we were able to utilize a fairly comprehensive register of corporations, associations and organizations, whether private or public, for-profit or nonprofit. This register, the SIRENE-File (*Système de repertoire des entreprises et des établissements*) lists the name, address, legal status, industrial classification code and number of employees of every French organization. Through a combination of legal status and classification code, it was possible to identify the great majority of French nonprofit organizations. This, in turn, allowed us to calculate the number of people employed in each ICNPO category. Using social security statistics (*Déclarations annuelle de données sociales*), it was then possible to estimate the average annual wage for different professional categories (professional, skilled, and unskilled workers) for each ICNPO group to yield the wage bill. Next we developed specific estimation procedures for each ICNPO group, to go from wage bill to operating expenditures, making use of satellite accounts for health and education, data available at government offices and nonprofit umbrella organizations, and otherwise utilizing special surveys that had been conducted to collect information on different types of nonprofit organizations. To gain information on giving and volunteering, we commissioned a representative population survey, which was carried out in 1991. For the revenue side, information from numerous public and nonprofit sources was put together, such as satellite accounts (for nonprofits working in the fields of health and education), social security statistics (for third-party payments), or data on international activities from the Ministry of Cooperation. For other sectors, we relied primarily on a survey of nonprofit organizations at the municipal level conducted by Viviane Mizrahi-Tchernonog (1992) at the Laboratoire d'Economie Sociale at the Sorbonne.

Germany

In (West) Germany, the Census of Work Places (*Arbeitsstätt-enzählung*) of 1987 provided the basic data on the number of establishments, in addition to data on full- and part-time jobs, key characteristics of the work force, and the total of gross wages and salaries. Unlike virtually all other countries, the industrial classification system in place in Germany until 1993 identified nonprofit establishments in the relevant industries as a separate category. With some adjustments, it was possible to line up the German SIC system with the ICNPO and derive the total employment base and wage bill for the German nonprofit sector in each major ICNPO group and subgroup as of 1987. These estimates were then updated to 1990 using social security statistics and related sources. Using industry-specific data from the Federal Statistical Office, available surveys on nonprofit organizations, and information provided by nonprofit umbrella organizations, we formulated industry-specific ratios for the relationship between wage bill, capital and operating expenditures in each ICNPO group and subgroup. We used a diverse set of sources (e.g., hospital and educational statistics; survey of sport clubs; foundation directories; and reports from various federal and state ministries) to collect information on the revenue side, and used data obtained from separate surveys of about 500 nonprofit organizations in East Germany and West Germany to estimate the share of each of the major revenue categories. In addition, we commissioned a population survey on giving and volunteering among the adult West German population in October 1992.

Hungary
Due to the changes that have occurred in Hungary in recent years, statistical reporting systems on nonprofit organizations are much less established than in other countries. Therefore, we relied almost exclusively on a sample survey of Hungarian nonprofit organizations that was carried out in May 1992. The sampling population consisted of all foundations and associations which were officially registered as of December 31, 1990. The sample was drawn separately for foundations (15.5% of the total number of foundations, N=284) and for associations (2.3% of the total number of registered associations, N=258). The foundation sample was then stratified by major ICNPO group, and the association sample by major ICNPO group and income category. With the help of a standardized survey form, data were collected in face-to-face interviews with representatives of the sampled organizations. Figures in this report represent population estimates based on the sample statistics, which have been corrected to take better account of the approximate size distribution of nonprofit organizations. The latter information was available from a broad-based survey of associations conducted by the Central Statistical Office in 1989. Given both the greater sampling error and the possibility of sampling bias at ICNPO subgroup levels, we report information for major groups only. The data for 1980 were estimated on the basis of the results of the 1970 and 1982 surveys on voluntary associations carried out by the Central Statistical Office.

Italy
In contrast to other developed market economies, no existing employment surveys nor any other baseline survey could be used as the basic building block for the estimation of nonprofit sector expenditures or revenues in Italy. In the absence of such statistics, the selected data assembly strategy represents a "bottom-up" approach whereby information was collected separately for each ICNPO group and subgroup. In general, this first involved the compilation of lists of nonprofit organizations at local, regional and national levels in an effort to reconstruct the approximate universe of establishments operating in a particular ICNPO field or industry. Standardized survey forms were then sent out to a sample (and sometimes the universe) of the establishments so identified. Data from the returned survey forms were then used to estimate the basic parameters for expenditure and revenue

items, using sector-specific estimation procedures that were validated by additional information obtained from statistical offices and umbrella organizations. Over 25 separate surveys were conducted, covering nonprofit museums, TV and radio stations, schools and universities, cultural associations, drug-addiction organizations, bands and choirs, social service providers and foundations, among others. In total, over 10,000 survey forms were sent out, of which 915 were returned.

Japan

The basic data for estimating the size, scope and revenue structure of the Japanese nonprofit sector was taken from a survey on private nonprofit organizations conducted by the Economic Planning Agency (*Minkan hieiri dantai jittai chosa hokoku*), which is used primarily for purposes of national income accounts. The survey, however, covers only parts of the nonprofit sector as defined by the structural-operational definition. While it includes civil law associations (*koeki hojin*) and some foundations, social welfare corporations, business and professional associations and unions, it does not cover health and education, nor a form of voluntary association called *nin'i dantai*. Moreover, the survey of nonprofit organizations also includes certain types of organizations that fall outside the scope of this study. Therefore, significant adjustments and additions had to be made to the data provided in the survey. This was done primarily by incorporating information available from other sources, such as the survey of social education and the survey on the financial condition of private schools from the Ministry of Education, Culture and Science; the survey of medical facilities from the Ministry of Health and Welfare; and more specialized sources such as surveys on consumer organizations, women's organizations, and philanthropic institutions, the latter completed by the Foundation Library Center of Japan. Some of these sources differed in the extent to which they identified nonprofit establishments; therefore, the exact estimation procedures differed somewhat by ICNPO group.

United Kingdom

In the United Kingdom, no general employment survey could be used as the baseline to estimate the size and scope of the nonprofit sector. Moreover, while data have been collected on parts of the sector, such as charities, on a routine basis, they tend to focus on income, revenue sources, and volunteering. The strategy for building up a statistical profile of the nonprofit sector was therefore to rely on existing data systems to the fullest extent possible and supplement these with original data to fill in the gaps. This, in turn, involved information obtained from various ministries and public agencies, umbrella organizations, survey statistics from previous research on specific types of nonprofit organizations, and local-level surveys to cross-validate existing statistics and to derive ratios for estimation procedures. By compiling revenue and expenditure figures for each ICNPO group and subgroup, estimates for the sector as a whole were built up in a step by step fashion. Larger surveys were conducted for two ICNPO groups covering environmental organizations and nonprofit organizations operating in the international arena.

United States

Data for the US nonprofit sector come primarily from Virginia Hodgkinson *et al.*, *Nonprofit Sector Almanac*, 1992–1993 (Washington, DC: Independent Sector, 1992), and were supplemented with data reported in Lester Salamon, *The Nonprofit Sector: A Primer* (New York: Foundation Center, 1992), the *Johns Hopkins Nonprofit Sector Project Survey*, Round III, and *Giving USA*. Since the employment data in the Almanac use headcount figures, these figures were converted to their full-time equivalent, based on the conversion ratios available from *Survey of Current Business* (August 1993, Tables 6.4c and 6.5c). The *Almanac* provides data organized by the SIC category as well by the NTEE classification. While there is rough correspondence between the largest categories of these systems and the ICNPO (such as health, education or social services), other categories (especially SIC 864 including a wide variety of civic associations) had to be disaggregated (using information provided in the NTEE classification that cross-cuts SIC) to fit the ICNPO categories. The revenue data in the *Almanac* were disaggregated to fit the revenue categories used in this project, based on revenue ratios available from the *Johns Hopkins Nonprofit Sector Project Survey*, Round III. For categories of organizations not available in that source, data from the *Almanac* and *Giving USA* were used.

Appendix D
Annual nonprofit sector operating expenditures by country and ICNPO group, 1990

Subsector/group	France	Germany	Hungary	Italy	Japan	United Kingdom	United States	Seven-country average
Culture, recreation	17.8	7.4	56.2	8.5	1.2	20.5	3.1	16.4
Education, research	24.8	11.9	4.0	21.7	39.5	42.4	22.7	23.9
Health	14.5	34.5	0.9	16.4	27.7	3.5	52.6	21.4
Social services	28.9	23.1	24.9	24.3	13.8	11.5	9.9	19.5
Environment	0.7	0.3	1.5	0.2	0.2	2.2	0.7	0.8
Development, housing	6.4	14.8	1.4	1.7	0.3	7.8	3.1	5.1
Civil, advocacy	2.9	1.1	0.4	2.2	0.9	0.7	0.3	1.2
Philanthropy	0.0	0.2	0.7	1.0	0.1	0.7	0.4	0.4
International	1.1	1.5	0.1	1.3	0.5	3.7	1.2	1.3
Business, professional	2.9	5.3	9.4	22.7	11.4	7.0	5.1	9.1
Other	0.0	0.0	0.5	0.0	4.5	0.0	0.9	2.0
	FF	DM	HUF	Lire	¥	£	$	
Total (millions)	216,649	86,808	25,922	26,059,197	13,716,653	26,352	346,355	—
Total (million U.S. $)	39,895	53,862	395	21,800	95,080	46,997	346,355	76,748
(million ECU)	31,335	42,304	310	17,122	74,678	36,913	272,035	60,280

Source: Johns Hopkins Comparative Nonprofit Sector Project

Appendix E

Employment in the nonprofit sector by country and ICNPO group, in percent, 1990

Subsector/group	France	Germany	Hungary	Italy	Japan	United Kingdom	United States	Seven-country average
Culture, recreation	11.4	6.3	64.0	4.4	1.1	27.7	3.5	16.9
Education, research	23.0	12.9	2.1	28.6	30.9	34.9	22.5	22.1
Health	17.0	35.8	0.2	14.2	37.1	4.6	47.0	22.3
Social services	38.4	32.3	16.3	35.2	19.4	15.4	14.4	24.5
Environment	0.6	0.2	0.8	0.2	0.2	1.8	1.1	0.7
Development, housing	4.7	6.0	0.2	4.6	0.3	7.8	6.0	4.2
Civic, advocacy	1.9	1.3	0.0	2.0	0.8	1.0	0.3	1.1
Philanthropy	0.0	0.3	0.3	0.5	0.1	0.8	0.3	0.3
International	1.1	0.5	0.0	1.5	0.3	2.4	—	1.0
Business, professional	1.9	4.4	14.2	8.8	6.3	3.7	3.4	6.1
Other	0.0	0.0	2.0	0.0	3.4	0.0	1.4	1.7
Total numbers	802,619	1,017,945	32,738	416,383	1,440,228	945,883	7,130,823	1,683,803

Note: Employment data are given in full-time equivalent

Source: Johns Hopkins Comparative Nonprofit Sector Project

149

Appendix F
Revenue sources of the nonprofit sector by country and ICNPO group, in percent, 1990

Subsector/group	France			Germany			Hungary		
	Private giving	Public sector payments	Private fees	Private giving	Public sector payments	Private fees	Private giving	Public sector payments	Private fees
Culture, recreation	4	41	55	9	17	74	19	31	49
Education, research	10	73	17	2	70	28	18	7	75
Health	8	84	8	3	84	13	61	19	20
Social services	5	60	35	7	83	10	22	12	66
Environment	15	32	52	4	23	73	0	95	5
Development, housing	2	37	61	0	57	43	57	16	28
Civic, advocacy	3	48	49	5	42	54	31	52	16
Philanthropy	51	5	44	1	15	85	71	25	4
International	66	22	12	17	77	6	73	0	27
Business, professional	8	16	76	0	5	94	12	1	87
Total	7	59	33	4	68	28	20	23	57

Subsector/group	Italy			Japan			United Kingdom		
	Private giving	Public sector payments	Private fees	Private giving	Public sector payments	Private fees	Private giving	Public sector payments	Private fees
Culture, recreation	10	22	68	4	13	84	7	11	81
Education, research	2	49	50	2	11	87	5	64	31
Health	2	72	27	0	96	4	26	23	51
Social services	7	60	33	0	65	35	40	26	35
Environment	14	22	64	10	4	85	36	19	45
Development, housing	2	28	70	0	24	76	4	58	38
Civic, advocacy	2	85	14	2	15	82	7	57	36
Philanthropy	41	7	52	23	2	75	20	28	52
International	5	81	14	13	24	63	39	38	23
Business, professional	0	0	100	0	11	89	2	1	97
Total	4	43	53	1	38	60	12	40	48

Subsector/group	United States			Seven-country average		
	Private giving	Public sector payments	Private fees	Private giving	Public sector payments	Private fees
Culture, recreation	27	17	57	11	22	67
Education, research	19	21	60	8	42	50
Health	9	36	55	15	59	25
Social services	28	51	21	16	51	33
Environment	27	44	29	15	34	51
Development, housing	19	40	41	12	37	51
Civic, advocacy	22	47	30	10	49	40
Philanthropy	32	0	68	34	12	54
International	31	50	19	38	39	23
Business, professional	0	0	100	3	5	92
Total	19	30	52	10	43	47

Source: Johns Hopkins Comparative Nonprofit Sector Project

REFERENCES

Aga Khan Foundation, "The Nairobi Statement," *Report of the Enabling Environment Conference: Effective Private Sector Contribution to Development in Sub-Saharan Africa.* Presented in Nairobi, Kenya, October 21–24, 1986 (Paris: Aga Khan Foundation, 1987).

Amenomori, Takayoshi, "Defining the Nonprofit Sector: Japan," in Lester M. Salamon and Helmut K. Anheier, eds., *Working Papers of the Johns Hopkins Comparative Nonprofit Sector Project*, No. 15 (Baltimore: The Johns Hopkins Institute for Policy Studies, 1993).

American Association of Fundraising Counsel, Inc., *Giving USA* (New York: American Association of Fundraising Counsel, various years).

Anheier, Helmut K., "An Elaborate Network: Profiling the Third Sector in Germany," in Benjamin Gidron, Ralph M. Kramer, and Lester M. Salamon, eds., *Government and the Third Sector: Emerging Relationships in Welfare States* (San Francisco: Jossey-Bass, 1992), pp. 31–56.

Anheier, Helmut K. and Wolfgang Seibel, "Defining the Nonprofit Sector: Germany," in Lester M. Salamon and Helmut K. Anheier, eds., *Working Papers of the Johns Hopkins Comparative Nonprofit Sector Project*, No. 6 (Baltimore: The Johns Hopkins Institute for Policy Studies, 1993).

Anheier, Helmut K., Gabriel Rudney, and Lester M. Salamon, "The Nonprofit Sector and the United Nations System of Accounts: Country Applications of SNA Guidelines," *Voluntas*, Vol. 4, No. 4 (1993), pp. 486–501.

Anheier, Helmut K. and Wolfgang Seibel, eds., *The Third Sector: Comparative Studies of Nonprofit Organizations* (Berlin: DeGruyter Publications, 1990).

Annis, S., "Can Small-Scale Development be a Large-Scale Policy? The Case of Latin America," *World Development*, Vol. 15, Supplement (1987), pp. 129–134.

Archambault, Edith, "Defining the Nonprofit Sector: France," in Lester

References

M. Salamon and Helmut K. Anheier, eds., *Working Papers of the Johns Hopkins Comparative Nonprofit Sector Project,* No. 7 (Baltimore: The Johns Hopkins Institute for Policy Studies, 1993).

Barbetta, Gian Paolo, "Defining the Nonprofit Sector: Italy," in Lester M. Salamon and Helmut K. Anheier, eds., *Working Papers of the Johns Hopkins Comparative Nonprofit Sector Project,* No. 8 (Baltimore: The Johns Hopkins Institute for Policy Studies, 1993).

Bratton, Michael, "Beyond the State: Civil Society and Associational Life in Africa," *World Politics* (April 1989), pp. 407–430.

Bundesverband Deutscher Stiftungen, *Verzeichnis der Deutschen Stiftungen* (Stuttgart: Hoppenstedt Verlag, 1991).

Central Intelligence Agency, *The World Factbook 1991* (Washington: Central Intelligence Agency, 1991).

Cheroutre, Marie-Thérèse, *Exercice et développement de la vie associative dans le cadre de la loi du 1er/07/1901* (Paris: Conseil Economique et Social, 1993).

Commission on Private Philanthropy and Public Needs (Filer Commission), *Giving in America* (Washington, D.C.: U.S. Government Printing Office, 1975).

Drabek, Anne Gordon, "Development Alternatives: The Challenge for NGOs," *World Development,* Vol. 15 (1987).

Dun & Bradstreet, *Principal International Businesses: The 1994 Marketing Directory* (Bethlehem, PA: Dun & Bradstreet Corporation, 1994).

Durning, A. B., "Action at the Grass-roots: Fighting Poverty and Environmental Decline," *Worldwatch Paper,* No. 88 (Washington, D.C.: Worldwatch Institute, 1989).

European Parliament, *Report of the Committee on Culture, Youth, Education and the Media on Foundations and Europe,* DOC EN / RR / 241 / 241238 (December 8, 1993), pp. 4–5.

Eurostat, "A statistical profile of the cooperative, mutual and nonprofit sector and its organisations in the European Community," *Services and Transport,* Theme 7, Series B, Short-term trends. Supplement 2 (1993).

Eurostat, *Social Protection Expenditures and Receipts, 1980–89* (Luxembourg: European Community, 1991).

Flora, Peter, "Introduction," in Peter Flora, ed., *Growth to Limits: The Western European Welfare States Since World War II,* Vol. I (Berlin: Walter deGruyter, 1986), pp. x–xxix.

Gidron, Benjamin, Ralph Kramer, and Lester M. Salamon, eds., *Government and the Third Sector: Emerging Relationships in Welfare States* (San Francisco: Jossey-Bass Publishers, 1992).

H.M. Home Office, *Profiting from Partnership: Efficiency Scrutiny of Government Funding of the Voluntary Sector,* prepared by Juliet Reisz, Richard

Boyce, Peter Collings, and Ross Hutchison (London: Her Majesty's Stationery Office, 1992).

Hodgkinson, Virginia A. and Murray S. Weitzman, *Giving and Volunteering in the United States* (Washington, D.C.: Independent Sector, 1992).

Hodgkinson, Virginia A., Murray S. Weitzman, Christopher M. Toppe, and Stephen M. Noga, *Nonprofit Almanac 1992–1993: Dimensions of the Independent Sector* (San Francisco: Jossey-Bass Publishers, 1992).

Hodgkinson, Virginia A. and Murray S. Weitzman, *Dimensions of the Independent Sector*, 3rd ed. (Washington, D.C.: Independent Sector, 1984).

Hopkins, Bruce, *The Law of Charitable Organizations* (New York: John A. Wiley and Sons, 1987).

International Labour Office, *The Cost of Social Security* (Geneva: International Labour Organization, 1993).

International Labour Office, *Year Book of Labour Statistics 1992* (Geneva: International Labour Organization, 1992).

James, Estelle, ed., *The Nonprofit Sector in International Perspective: Studies in Comparative Culture and Policy* (Oxford: Oxford University Press, 1989).

James, Estelle, "The Nonprofit Sector in Comparative Perspective," in Walter W. Powell, ed., *The Nonprofit Sector: A Research Handbook* (New Haven: Yale University Press, 1987).

Johnson, Norman, *The Welfare State in Transition: The Theory and Practice of Welfare Pluralism* (Amherst: The University of Massachusetts Press, 1987).

Kandil, Amani, "Defining the Nonprofit Sector: Egypt," in Lester M. Salamon and Helmut K. Anheier, eds., *Working Papers of the Johns Hopkins Comparative Nonprofit Sector Project*, No. 10 (Baltimore: The Johns Hopkins Institute for Policy Studies, 1993).

Kendall, Jeremy and Martin Knapp, "Defining the Nonprofit Sector: The United Kingdom," in Lester M. Salamon and Helmut K. Anheier, eds., *Working Papers of the Johns Hopkins Comparative Nonprofit Sector Project*, No. 5 (Baltimore: The Johns Hopkins Institute for Policy Studies, 1993).

Kouchner, B., ed., *Les nouvelles solidarités* (Paris: Presses Universitaires de France, 1990).

Kuti, Éva, "Defining the Nonprofit Sector: Hungary," in Lester M. Salamon and Helmut K. Anheier, eds., *Working Papers of the Johns Hopkins Comparative Nonprofit Sector Project*, No. 13 (Baltimore: The Johns Hopkins Institute for Policy Studies, 1993).

Landim, Leilah, "Defining the Nonprofit Sector: Brazil," in Lester M. Salamon and Helmut K. Anheier, eds., *Working Papers of the Johns Hopkins Comparative Nonprofit Sector Project*, No. 9 (Baltimore: The Johns Hopkins Institute for Policy Studies, 1993).

References

Mabbott, John, *Improving Government Funding: Report and Recommendations* (London: National Council for Voluntary Organisations, 1992).

McCarthy, Kathleen, Virginia Hodgkinson, and Russy Sumariwalla, *The Nonprofit Sector in the Global Community* (San Francisco: Jossey-Bass Publishers, 1992).

Mizrahi-Tchernonog, Viviane, "Municipal Subsidies to French Associations," *Voluntas* 3(3) (1992): 351–364.

Nisbet, Robert, *Community and Power*, 2d ed. (New York: Oxford University Press, 1962).

Organization for Economic Cooperation and Development Statistics Directorate, *National Accounts 1980–1992* (Paris: OECD, 1994).

Organization for Economic Cooperation and Development, *Economic Surveys 1991, France* (Paris: OECD, 1991).

Organization for Economic Cooperation and Development, *Economic Surveys 1991, Germany* (Paris: OECD, 1991).

Organization for Economic Cooperation and Development, *Economic Surveys 1991, Hungary* (Paris: OECD, 1991).

Organization for Economic Cooperation and Development, *Economic Surveys 1991, Italy* (Paris: OECD, 1991).

Organization for Economic Cooperation and Development, *Economic Surveys 1991, Japan* (Paris: OECD, 1991).

Organization for Economic Cooperation and Development, *Economic Surveys 1991, United Kingdom* (Paris: OECD, 1991).

Organization for Economic Cooperation and Development, *Economic Surveys 1991, United States* (Paris: OECD, 1991).

Organization for Economic Cooperation and Development, *National Accounts, Detailed Tables, 1976–1988* (Paris: OECD, 1991), Table 9.

Organization for Economic Cooperation and Development, *The Welfare State in Crisis* (Paris: OECD, 1981).

Pongsapich, Amara, "Defining the Nonprofit Sector: Thailand," in Lester M. Salamon and Helmut K. Anheier, eds., *Working Papers of the Johns Hopkins Comparative Nonprofit Sector Project*, No. 11 (Baltimore: The Johns Hopkins Institute for Policy Studies, 1993).

Rudney, Gabriel and Murray S. Weitzman, "Significance of Employment and Earnings Trends in the Philanthropic Sector," in *PONPO Working Paper* (New Haven: Program on Nonprofit Organizations, 1983).

Salamon, Lester M., *The Invisible Sector: The Nonprofit Sector in an Era of Retrenchment* (Chicago: University of Chicago Press, forthcoming).

Salamon, Lester M., *Partners in Public Service: Government and the Nonprofit Sector in the Modern Welfare State* (Baltimore: Johns Hopkins University Press, 1994).

Salamon, Lester M., "The Rise of the Nonprofit Sector," *Foreign Affairs*, Vol. 73, No. 4 (1994), pp. 111–124.

References

Salamon, Lester M., "The Marketization of Welfare: Changing Nonprofit and For-Profit Roles in the American Welfare State," *Social Service Review*, Vol. 67, No. 1 (March 1993), pp. 17–39.

Salamon, Lester M., *America's Nonprofit Sector: A Primer* (New York: The Foundation Center, 1992).

Salamon, Lester M., "The Voluntary Sector and the Future of the Welfare State," *Nonprofit and Voluntary Sector Quarterly*, Vol. XVIII, No. 1 (Spring 1989), pp. 11–24.

Salamon, Lester M., *Beyond Privatization: The Tools of Government Action* (Washington, D.C.: The Urban Institute Press, 1989).

Salamon, Lester M., "Of Market Failure, Government Failure, and Third-Party Government: Toward a Theory of Government-Nonprofit Relations in the Modern Welfare State," *Journal of Voluntary Action Research*, Vol. 16, Nos. 1–2 (January–June 1987), pp. 29–49.

Salamon, Lester M., "Rethinking Public Management: Third-Party Government and the Changing Forms of Public Action," *Public Policy*, Vol. 29, No. 3 (1981), pp. 255–275.

Salamon, Lester M. and Alan J. Abramson, *The Federal Budget and the Nonprofit Sector* (Washington, D.C.: The Urban Institute Press, 1982).

Salamon, Lester M. and Helmut K. Anheier, eds., *Defining the Nonprofit Sector: A Cross-National Analysis* (Manchester: Manchester University Press, 1996).

Salamon, Lester M. and Helmut K. Anheier, "Caring Sector or Caring Society? Discovering the Nonprofit Sector Cross-Nationally," in Paul Schervisch, Virginia Hodgkinson and Margaret Gates and Associates, eds., *Care and Community in Modern Society* (San Francisco: Jossey-Bass Publishers, 1995).

Salamon, Lester M. and Helmut K. Anheier, "The Third Route: Subsidiarity, Third-Party Government and the Provision of Social Services in the United States and Germany," *ILE Notebook*, No. 19 (Paris: OECD, 1994).

Salamon, Lester M. and Helmut K. Anheier, "In Search of the Nonprofit Sector I: The Question of Definitions," *Voluntas*, Vol. 3, No. 2 (1992), pp. 125–151.

Salamon, Lester M. and Helmut K. Anheier, "In Search of the Nonprofit Sector II: The Problem of Classification," *Voluntas*, Vol. 3, No. 3 (1992), pp. 267–309.

Santos, Wanderley Guilherme, *Publico e Privado no Sistema Brasileiro* [Public and Private in the Brazilian System] (Rio de Janeiro, 1990), mimeographed.

Sen, Siddhartha, "Defining the Nonprofit Sector: India," in Lester M. Salamon and Helmut K. Anheier, eds., *Working Papers of the Johns Hopkins Comparative Nonprofit Sector Project*, No. 12 (Baltimore: The Johns Hopkins Institute for Policy Studies, 1993).

References

Taylor, Marilyn, "The Changing Role of the Nonprofit Sector in Britain: Moving Toward the Market," in Benjamin Gidron, Ralph Kramer and Lester M. Salamon, eds., *Government and the Nonprofit Sector: Emerging Relationships in Welfare States* (San Francisco: Jossey-Bass Publishers, 1992), pp. 147–175.

Taylor, Marilyn, *Directions for the Next Decade: Understanding Social and Institutional Trends* (London: National Council for Voluntary Organisations, 1990).

Tice, Helen Stone, "The Nonprofit Sector in a National Accounts Framework," *Voluntas*, Vol. 4, No. 4 (1993), pp. 445–464.

U.S. Census Bureau, *1977 Census of Service Industries* (Washington, D.C.: U.S. Government Printing Office, 1981).

United Nations, *System of National Accounts 1993* (Brussels/Luxembourg, New York, Paris, Washington, DC: Commission of the European Communities, International Monetary Fund, Organization for Economic Cooperation and Development, United Nations, and World Bank, 1993).

United Nations Department for Economic and Social Information and Policy Analysis, *Demographic Yearbook* (New York: United Nations, 1992).

United Nations Educational Scientific and Cultural Organization (UNESCO), *Statistical Yearbook 1991* (Paris: United Nations Educational Scientific and Cultural Organization, 1991).

United Nations Statistical Office, *National Accounts Statistics: Main Aggregates and Detailed Tables 1988* (New York: United Nations, 1990).

Uphoff, Norman, "Assisted Self-Reliance: Working With, Rather than for, the Poor," in John P. Lewis, ed., *Strengthening the Poor* (New Brunswick: Transaction Books, 1988), pp. 47–60.

Weisbrod, Burton, *The Voluntary Nonprofit Sector* (Lexington, MA: Lexington Books, 1978).

World Bank, *World Development Report 1992* (New York: Oxford University Press, 1992).

Zerubavel, Eviatar, *The Fine Line* (Chicago: University of Chicago Press, 1991).

PROJECT PUBLICATIONS

Working papers

1. Salamon, Lester M. and Helmut K. Anheier, "Toward an Understanding of the International Nonprofit Sector."
2. Salamon, Lester M. and Helmut K. Anheier, "In Search of the Nonprofit Sector I: The Question of Definitions."
3. Salamon, Lester M. and Helmut K. Anheier, "In Search of the Nonprofit Sector II: The Problem of Classification."
4. Anheier, Helmut K., Gabriel Rudney, and Lester M. Salamon, "The Nonprofit Sector in the United Nations System of National Accounts: Definition, Treatment, and Practice."
5. Jeremy Kendall and Martin Knapp, "Defining the Nonprofit Sector: United Kingdom."
6. Anheier, Helmut K. and Wolfgang Seibel, "Defining the Nonprofit Sector: Germany."
7. Archambault, Edith, "Defining the Nonprofit Sector: France."
8. Barbetta, Gian Paolo, "Defining the Nonprofit Sector: Italy."
9. Landim, Leilah, "Defining the Nonprofit Sector: Brazil."
10. Kandil, Amani, "Defining the Nonprofit Sector: Egypt."
11. Pongsapich, Amara, "Defining the Nonprofit Sector: Thailand."
12. Sen, Siddhartha, "Defining the Nonprofit Sector: India."
13. Kuti, Éva, "Defining the Nonprofit Sector: Hungary."
14. Atingdui, Lawrence, "Defining the Nonprofit Sector: Ghana."
15. Amenomori, Takayoshi, "Defining the Nonprofit Sector: Japan."
16. Lundström, Tommy and Filip Wijkström, "Defining the Nonprofit Sector: Sweden."
17. Salamon, Lester M. and Helmut K. Anheier, "Caring Sector or Caring Society? Discovering the Nonprofit Sector Cross-Nationally."

159

Project publications

Books

Anheier, Helmut K. and Salamon, Lester M., eds., *The Nonprofit Sector in the Developing World* (Manchester: Manchester University Press).

Anheier, Helmut K. and Wolfgang Seibel, *The Nonprofit Sector in Germany* (Manchester: Manchester University Press).

Archambault, Edith, *The Nonprofit Sector in France* (Manchester: Manchester University Press).

Barbetta, Gian Paolo, *The Nonprofit Sector in Italy* (Manchester: Manchester University Press).

Kendall, Jeremy and Martin Knapp, *The Nonprofit Sector in the United Kingdom* (Manchester: Manchester University Press).

Kuti, Éva, *The Nonprofit Sector in Hungary* (Manchester: Manchester University Press).

Salamon, Lester M., *The Nonprofit Sector in the United States* (Manchester: Manchester University Press).

Salamon, Lester M. and Helmut K. Anheier, *Defining the Nonprofit Sector: a cross-national analysis* (Manchester: Manchester University Press).

Salamon, Lester M. and Helmut K. Anheier, *The Emerging Nonprofit Sector: a comparative analysis* (Manchester, UK: Manchester University Press).

Yamamoto, Tadashi, *The Nonprofit Sector in Japan* (Manchester: Manchester University Press).

INDEX